A Tribute to Walter

Walter Wangerin Jr. died on August 5, 2021, while this book was in its final stages of editing and production. You can learn more about this remarkable pastor, author, and teacher at walterwangerinjr.org and discover his numerous books. The following excerpts were written by his friend, best-selling author Philip Yancey, in "My Benediction to the Beloved Storyteller, Walter Wangerin Jr." (Christianity Today, August 9, 2021). These comments are provided with Philip's gracious permission.

"As both a sermonizer and an artist, with graduate degrees in theology and English, Walt lived with the constant tension of how best to express themes of grace and the cross. As a pastor, he found that *story* conveys truth most effectively and profoundly. As he told one interviewer, 'While the intellect must be addressed in communicating Christian truth, it will not be truth for the hearer until the hearer is also touched deep within himself or herself.'

"Walt knew he was swimming against the tide. He spoke of the 'cool pragmatism' of modern literary taste. He sought instead to draw the reader into another world, a suspension of disbelief carried more by music and lyricism than by sense and reason. He once told me in a letter that 'a writer hopes for the obedience of a good reader who says, "I will enter this world a while, however different it is from my own more familiar expressions of truth."'

"Rest content, dear Walter. You have given us a well-crafted life. Because you paid attention, so can we."

Praise for *Storycraft*

"Preachers want hearers to experience the good news the way Dietrich Bonhoeffer described it: as Christ walking among the congregation as the Word today. In this book, Walt Wangerin Jr. teaches us to draw upon the stories of Scripture, the breadth of literature, and the stories of ministry, and then consider the important fine details of how we embody our preaching. He graciously invites us into his life, ministry, and legacy to show us why we experience great stories and great preaching as gospel events that transform lives."

—Dee Pederson, bishop,
Southwestern Minnesota Synod, ELCA

"Wangerin's *Storycraft* is unique among books describing the role of stories in preaching. He explores the power of story through the art of telling stories. In doing so, he strikes the perfect balance of reason and art. With simple and singular clarity, he guides the reader in creating and classifying stories. With wide-ranging glimpses of story and poetry, he invites the reader to explore the mystery of this art."

—David Schmitt, Benidt Memorial Professor of Homiletics
and Literature, Concordia Seminary. St. Louis

storycraft

storycraft

THE ART OF
Spiritual Narrative

Walter Wangerin Jr.
Foreword by Frederick Niedner

Fortress Press
Minneapolis

STORYCRAFT
The Art of Spiritual Narrative

Copyright © 2022 Fortress Press, an imprint of 1517 Media. All rights reserved. Except for brief quotations in critical articles or reviews, no part of this book may be reproduced in any manner without prior written permission from the publisher. Email copyright@1517.media or write to Permissions, Fortress Press, PO Box 1209, Minneapolis, MN 55440-1209.

All Scripture quotations, unless otherwise indicated, are from the New Revised Standard Version Bible, copyright © 1989 National Council of the Churches of Christ in the United States of America. Used by permission. All rights reserved worldwide.

Scripture quotations marked (ESV) are from the ESV® Bible (The Holy Bible, English Standard Version®), copyright © 2001 by Crossway, a publishing ministry of Good News Publishers. Used by permission. All rights reserved.

Scripture quotations marked (NKJV) are from the New King James Version®. Copyright © 1982 by Thomas Nelson. Used by permission. All rights reserved.

Scripture quotations marked (NASB) are from the (NASB®) New American Standard Bible®, Copyright © 1960, 1971, 1977, 1995, 2020 by The Lockman Foundation. Used by permission. All rights reserved. www.lockman.org

Scripture quotations marked (KJV) are from the King James Version.

"The Parrot" copyright © 1965 by Carmen Bernos De Gasztold. Originally published by Viking Penguin Inc. Currently published in *The Creatures Choir*. Reprinted by permission of Curtis Brown, Ltd.

Cover design: John Lucas, LucasArt.com

Print ISBN: 978-1-5064-8175-3
eBook ISBN: 978-1-5064-8176-0

Fain would I draw nigh,
Fain put thee on, exchanging my lay-sword
For that of th' holy Word.

—George Herbert, "The Priesthood"

Contents

Foreword — ix
Prologue: Preliminary Comments — xi

PART I:
The Effect of a Told Story

1. How Children and Adults Enter the Story — 3
2. Lily — 11
3. What Does Faith Have to Do with It? — 25
4. Right Ways and Wrong Ways to Tell a Children's Story — 29
5. Naming I — 33
6. Naming II — 37

PART II:
To Build a Story

7. Composing a Story Step by Step — 45
8. Making Our Stories Feel Real — 53
9. Spiritual Preparation — 61

PART III:
Six Sorts of Stories

10. Stories of Illustration — 67
11. Stories about the Presence and the Work of a Transforming God — 73
12. Personal Histories — 83
13. Factual Historical Stories — 93

| 14 | The Jewish Haggadah | 97 |
| 15 | Stories That Compose an Entire Sermon | 103 |

PART IV:
Theatrics

16	Theatrical Preachers in the Past	119
17	Motion and Meaning I	121
18	Motion and Meaning II	127
19	The Entrance	131
20	Preacher as Actor, Sermon as Play Script	135

Notes   149

Foreword

Among the many volumes that have analyzed the role of "story" in contemporary preaching and teaching in the church or have sought to teach preachers and teachers how best to use stories, this book offers a theology of preaching in a language that isn't specially coded for professionals in some guild or inner circle. It tells about the Word of God incarnated and how that Word takes on flesh and bone today in the practiced speech, the physical presence, and the context of loving service offered up by those who preach. Words, whether human or divine, define, shape, and call things into being. For better or worse, stories made up of words create worlds in which trusting listeners live and work. This book helps those who would proclaim gospel understanding and trust in the power of their words and the ways in which the Word gives life to those who listen and believe.

This book contains many examples of the kinds of stories that preachers and communities have told and inhabited and by which they have found their way, from tales of personal experience to brief poems to ancient classics to stories that crack open and find meanings in older stories that have long lain dormant. It offers a provocative anthology of narrative types and helps one rediscover the riches of the past and perhaps even discover a "pearl of great price" in one's own experience.

Wangerin offers here a manual for a preacher's crafting and use of stories, and after a lifetime of preparing and preaching sermons, as well as receiving and carefully observing other's preaching, he also helpfully examines aspects of preaching that books on homiletics seldom discuss. In this book, he invites preachers to examine and understand the weaknesses and strengths of the preaching personas they employ "on stage" as they proclaim.

Dr. Frederick Niedner

Prologue

Preliminary Comments

In *Performing the Word*, Dr. Jana Childers refers to Albert Mehrabian's observation that when people speak face-to-face, they communicate their thoughts by more than 55 percent of their bodily actions, 39 percent by their tones of voice, and a mere 7 percent by the words themselves.[1] This is, of course, an extreme exaggeration. Yet it points to the general ways by which we preachers can communicate—theatrics.

Mehrabian's observation is contemporary. Saint Augustine preached in the fifth century, now and again performing while he did. It was, in those days, the custom for a preacher or a teacher to sit in the chancel while the assembled people stood to listen. But Augustine would sometimes stand up and walk among them, touching a shoulder and speaking in fatherly tones, but sometimes he would speak in a scolding tone, rebuking the oblivious, those who were eating their lunches, scattering crumbs on the floor, or others who were chitchatting, gossiping with their neighbors. He is said to have thundered at these blockheads that they dishonored Christ himself even as Christ's words were reverberating among them in the church.

The bishop's body was visible and expressive so that the people could *experience* his sermons.

Regarding the way our congregations might come to experience our stories and our sermons, Robert Hughes and Robert Kysar write,

Theological reflection . . . will be concrete and specific rather than abstract and general. Having spoken of the general, overarching framework for life's experience, we need to recognize that the gospel framework is powerfully known and experienced only as it is enfleshed in concrete and specific language. The listener has to be helped to see the way in which the sermon's message is lived out. . . . The preacher shows the listeners real life in situations in which grace is experienced and shared.[2]

In his relatively brief book *The Portal of Beauty: Towards a Theology of Aesthetics*, Bruno Forte observes that "in the symbols, we are given to experience more meaning than can be articulated or understood; new perspectives of thought and life are invoked. . . . The ideal does not absorb the real, but must recognize that the real far surpasses in power so as to open itself and go beyond itself towards ever wider horizons."[3]

Now and again throughout this book, I will tell versions of my own personal experiences. Though there will be a historical core to my memory of the events, the further they recede into the past, the more will I, as others, add unremembered or invented details that, nonetheless, give voice to the emotions of those past events. This is captured by Brenda Miller and Suzanne Paola, who write, "We continually—often unconsciously—renovate our memories, shaping them into stories that bring coherence out of chaos."[4]

PART I

The Effect of a Told Story

Reader, my story ends in freedom.

—Anonymous, *Incidents in the Life of a Slave Girl*

1

How Children and Adults Enter the Story

The effect of a *told* story is not like the effect of the stories that individuals read silently in their minds. They remain isolated and separated from their communities. But a story told out loud becomes the congregation's *experience*. The listeners dwell in it as though it were a house, and it becomes their real and personal experience when their senses are engaged.

Vladimir Nabokov writes in his *Lectures on Literature*, "We must see things and hear things, we must visualize the rooms, the clothes, the manners of an author's people. The color of Fanny Price's eyes in *Mansfield Park* and the furnishings of her cold little room."[1]

A human voice acknowledges the humanity of those who listen.

A relationship—call it a covenant—is established between us (the preacher) and our people (the congregation). Together, we form a living community. Over time, and by the many stories we've told our congregations over and over again, we can earn their trust. They are ready to give us their hearts, their minds, and their full attention.

Our tales will often comfort or delight our people. But we shouldn't avoid the stories that contain evils, such as the dangers that Christians must endure as well as the sins that they have committed. For, believing in our trustworthiness, they will allow themselves to experience our judgments because they also believe in grace and forgiveness, knowing that all things will come round right in the end.

T. S. Eliot writes in his essay "A Dialogue on Dramatic Poetry," "If we are religious, then we shall only be aware of the Mass as art. . . . [But] a devout person, assisting at Mass, is not in the frame of mind of a person attending a drama, for he [or she] is participating."

Eliot continues, "In participating we are supremely conscious of certain realities, and unconscious of others. . . . We cannot be aware solely of divine realities. We must also be aware of human realities."[2]

Thus Eliot teaches the story's effect upon its hearers. Their participation, as I've indicated above, becomes an experience that can change them.

What began as a curiosity ends in faith.

Likewise, Aristotle taught that the experiences instilled in his audience changed them not only by what they heard but also by what they saw—stories performed on the stage of a vast Greek theater.

Tragedy inspires both pity and fear.

It has been my Sunday custom to arrive at church before dawn and then to pace up and down the aisle to find and refresh and finish the words and phrases of the sermon ahead.

One Sunday morning, Rita Cooksey, a member of my congregation, surprised me by arriving half an hour before the worship service. Rita is a tall, slender, young African American woman whose complexion has the rich color of polished walnut.

"What you gonna preach, Rev?" she asked, and I answered, "The Good Samaritan."

"Ooo, a story!" she said. "It'll curl my toes."

Stories will do that to you.

In his book *The Uses of Enchantment,* Bruno Bettelheim writes, "Literary critics such as G. K. Chesterton and C. S. Lewis felt that fairy stories are 'spiritual explorations,' and hence 'the most life-like' because they reveal 'human life as seen, or felt, or divined from the inside.'"[3]

Living within a story, then, individuals can become one of its characters, and their experience is made complete. I count seven stages by which a child, lying in bed before she falls asleep, listens to her mother as she reads a good fairy tale. It is no different for a congregation on a Sunday morning. Stories make children of us all.

1. At first, the tale is a pleasant diversion. It isn't "real." It acts like a sort of school recess for children otherwise busy with their books. Just so are the stories that a pastor tells. They too offer a break from the hectic and even the mortal events in their lives.

2. The listener begins to recognize that there are general truths in the story and that they have a universal value, and in spite of its fantasies, it accords with her own personal experiences. "Yes," she says, "people are like that." At this level, the congregation leans forward in expectation. It's important to realize that ours is a rational act, an effort to help our people *understand* its meaning but not yet experience it.

3. Now, whether they are children or a church of listening adults, they become conscious of their own selfhoods because they have become aware that there are parallels between their individual selves and the characters in the story. This relationship is like a mirror in which they see themselves, even though they remain *outside* and yet not *inside* the tale. Nevertheless, the story is the beginning of a personal identity, though there still remains a film, something like a sheet of Saran Wrap, separating the listener from the tale's characters. The story is still a story.

4. This stage is the pivot, a transition, and a choice. It can happen in an instant or else over a period of time as the tale is

repeated. When the listeners are ready, they make their choices, albeit unconsciously. Theirs is a discrete act, proof of an emerging and independent personhood. The living covenant is, now, established between the tale and the self.

And the transition? The listeners release themselves into the story. Each becomes one of its characters, perhaps the sly, self-saving Hansel and Gretel; or that hero Jack the Giant Killer; or Cinderella, to whom the birds threw down a most beautiful gown—the Holy Spirit who hovered over her with blessings.

It may frustrate a child's parents when she asks to hear the same story told over and over again. They think that stories should always be new because they and the child already know how the story ends. But it is by repetition that the child moves step by step ever deeper into the story.

Likewise, we preachers should not limit ourselves to telling a story only once. Rather, we ought to repeat it twice or three times a year, each time with a variation.

One time is dismissible. Three times is an invitation.

5. Now both children and adults in their pews have accepted the story's experiential effects. They wear the story and its characters like gloves.

They are the pilgrim in John Bunyan's *Pilgrim's Progress*. Their names are "Christian." As Christian, they fall into the Slough of Despond. But in the end, Christian reaches the Celestial City, where he receives a letter that says, "Hail! I bring thee good tidings that the master calleth for thee." His last words can also be ours: "I come, Lord, to be with thee, and bless thee."

For preachers and their people, the story does not require the suspension of disbelief. It is the present shape and the behavior of *all* belief.

6. At this point, the listeners have lost consciousness of an external listening and are experiencing self. No longer do they "wear the story like a glove," for they have accomplished the

essential goal toward which the story has led them. They *are* what they experience.

7. Finally, a person and persons emerge from the story as if from a house into the light of a common day—but changed. They are Easter's butterfly, emerging from its chrysalis. The world was a chaos when they entered the house, entered the story. But having experienced it, now the world has become a cosmos.

My wife and I adopted an eighteen-month-old child. Her birth father was Black and her birth mother white. Her complexion was the color of a cup of tea—what used to be called "high yaller." Her hair was straight, but her features had the cast of an African American. As she grew, she suffered the scorn of Black children and the rejection of white adults.

To persuade our daughter that she had an intrinsic value and a personal worth, I told her the story of God's creation with embellishments for herself alone.

"On the second day, God said," I said, "'I am going to make a child, and I am going to love my child, and I am going to protect her from all the dangers and the devils above the sky.'

"So God went up to the highest of high and made a hard, blue dome and called it 'Sky' and named the vast and endless oceans 'Sea.'

"And God said, 'The child whom I'm going to love will not be able to swim.'

"So the Creator caused a dry land to rise out of the sea, a land as wide as the world, and named it 'Earth.'"

My girl-child had just entered kindergarten. She was lying in bed. I was sitting on the side of it. I paused and stroked her cheek.

Then I said, "This isn't the end of your story, because God hadn't yet created you."

I continued, saying, "The great, almighty God said, 'My child must never, never be lonely.'

"So the Lord God walked to the edge of the sea and said, 'Swarm!'

"Suddenly, thousands of every kind of fish were swimming in the water: sharks and whales and swordfish and flying fish and trout and—way, way out in the ocean—a huge creature named Leviathan, and God laughed at its playfulness.

"Then your maker stood on a high mountain and shouted to the sky, 'Swarm!'

"Suddenly, thousands of every kind of bird were flying and circling and swooping: hawks, sparrows chasing crows away from their nests, red-breasted robins, and eagles on their wide and wonderful wings.

"You know that it took seven days to create the world. But maybe you don't know that on the sixth day, God said, 'I don't want my child to be lonely,' and therefore made animals—cows and sheep and horses and humpbacked camels and rats and cats and dogs and dingoes. And the wolves lay snuggled with lambs, and lions lay down with baby calves."

Finally, "Here it is, Girl! Here's the best part of your story! God said, 'It's time! It's time to make my little girl.'

"Think about how Mommy bakes bread to light brown and crackling crust. That's the color that God gave to your skin. And then what? Well, *this* what is a doozy. God leaned down, and it seemed that the great Creator was going to kiss you. Yes, but this was so much more than a kiss. It was the breath, it was the spirit of the Holy One, and you too came to life!

"Then you looked up at the blue bowl of Sky, and you smiled, and you said, 'God made that just for me.' Then you looked down at the earth and at the fish and at the birds and at the animals, and you said, 'So many friends!'

"And you were—no, you *are*—just like God. You are so important that it doesn't matter when kids scorn you or when adults turn away. That's going to change because you are the apple of God's eye."

It seemed to her mother and me that our daughter had been brought to life for a second time. So we named her Talitha. "Child, arise."

In a well-told story, the listeners lose their sense of real time and live in the all-encompassing time of the story. It's like this: when we're sitting in a theater, lost in the story of a fascinating movie, it takes us out of ticktock time and into its timeless time, and when we exit the theater, we are surprised to find that the day has become the evening.

It's the same when we preachers are telling a biblical story. It too can collapse all time into a universal time. The past and the present are one.

Witness Deuteronomy 5:2–5, when Moses, in his 120th year, stands on Mount Nebo giving his last address to the Israelites, saying, "The Lord our God made a covenant with us in Horeb" (Deut 5:2 ESV).

Us? That "us" is chronologically impossible. The people of this generation were never slaves in Egypt or brought out of the land by the Lord, for the previous generation had died in the wilderness.

Nevertheless, Moses says, "Not with our fathers did the Lord make this covenant, but with *us*, who are all of us here alive today. The Lord spoke with you face to face at the mountain, out of the midst of the fire" (Deut 5:3–5 ESV; italics mine).

In Hebrew, Moses's words have a rhythmic, liturgical effect, which indicates that they were, and are still, recited by the Jews.

Again, "Not with our fathers . . . but with us, who are all of us here alive."

How can the impossible become the possible?

By the Hebrews' and then the Jews' sense of a sacred story. The very telling makes its time, as I've said, *all* time, and those who hear it are in the past and in the present both at once, for there is neither *there* nor *here*. And *all* faithful people living on the earth receive a divine validation.

It is the same with our Eucharist. When we tell our sacred story—though not with its full history or with its many details but reduced to a few phrases—we speak and perform our holy and ritualistic mystery with a few phrases: "In the night when he was betrayed the Lord took bread," thus collapsing all time into one time. We are the disciples who ate (*we* eat) and drank (*we* drink) the body and the blood of Christ with the apostles, the martyrs, and the believers and all the company of heaven.

Of course. The spirit of the Lord Jesus Christ is omnipresent.

2

Lily

The story I'm about to tell is long and complicated. Nevertheless, I was able to make it the entirety of my sermon without commentary or explanations. A congregation can come to feel what it experiences. I entitled this story "Lily" because Lily is its protagonist.

From 1974 to the late 1980s, I served a small, inner-city, African American congregation in Evansville, Indiana.

Its sanctuary could seat no more than 120 people shoulder to shoulder in eleven pews. This was the only real room on the main floor.

The church's lower floor was the same size as the sanctuary above. There were a kitchen and two lavatories and a boiler room and a central space for the congregation's assemblies, chit-chat and coffee after a service, and potluck meals.

Six steps up from the lower floor and six steps down from the upper met on a small landing with doors for entering and exiting.

One cold Sunday evening on the twentieth of December 1981, I drove our children's choir (the Grace Notes) to St. Mary's Hospital to sing Christmas carols to members who lay sick—especially to Miz Odessa Williams, who lay at death's door. The children had never laid eyes on her before. What they saw now was an old, cadaverous Black woman whose arms and legs looked like broom handles under the sheet and whose fingers were knuckled and as thin and long as pencils. Her breath smelled of physical corruption. The small, incandescent light bulb above the head of her bed showed that her once brown face had become chalky with deep wrinkles scoring her face with the history of a long life lived.

The children divided into two little groups and crept to either side of her bed. They gawked. They shifted from foot to foot, for the sight and the smells unnerved them.

Miz Odessa Williams was dying of lung cancer.

Mary, my seven-year-old daughter, stood across the bed from me, looking solemnly down at the old woman.

Dee Dee Lawrence—like my daughter, seven years old—stood at the foot of the bed. This spherical child had been blessed with an angelic soprano and an enchanting and soaring descant.

The children did not, and perhaps *could* not, speak.

I asked, "What's the matter? Cat got your tongues? Sing for Miz Odessa. That's why we've come."

Mary said, "She won't hear us."

"It doesn't matter," I responded. "Maybe she can't hear you with her ears. But I think she'll hear you with her heart. Sing, I don't know, 'Away in a Manger.'"

Timmy Moore started to murmur the carol in his couch-comfortable voice. He had gotten to "the little Lord Jesus" when Dee Dee made a duet with him. And finally, the rest of the children joined in. The camaraderie strengthened the voices.

Odessa's eyes fluttered open. When the Grace Notes saw that, their own eyes began to sparkle.

And Miz Williams started to frown. Then it seemed that she was chewing something delicious, gumming it with her toothless mouth. The children knew what it meant when an old Black woman chewed and frowned. This was how she showed her pleasure.

So then they harked the herald angels.

They sweetened the scent in the room by singing about that little town of Bethlehem.

Another carol, and another. And then I said, "Dee Dee? 'Silent Night.'"

Oh, that dear, round-faced girl! There arose from her throat the sound of a song sparrow: "Silent night, holy night."

Odessa's eyes flicked left and right, searching for the source of the nightingale. She found it at the foot of her bed.

Dee Dee alone. Dee Dee singing solo: "Shepherds quake at the sight . . ."

Now Miz Odessa Williams raised her bony arms and became Dee Dee's choir director, and the small girl trusted the old woman completely.

Odessa lifted Dee Dee as a bird in flight. And higher and higher until the bird flew up through the ceiling and out into the night, and she rang the bells in heaven.

I could hardly stand the silvery sound of this celestial child.

Miz Williams sent her soaring to the stars.

Dee Dee's eyelids fluttered as she sang.

Then, "Jesus, Lord at your birth." Gently, now, and by meek degrees, Odessa lowered the girl down and down to earth. "Jesus, Lord at thy birth," and the hospital room breathed a silent joy.

I said, "OK. Time to go home."

But no one moved.

The children were gazing at Odessa with expressions of expectation. They'd come to feel that she had been their grandmother all their lives long.

And their expectations were fulfilled, for the woman began to preach.

"Oh, Chirren," she said in a voice that sounded like the cracking of a bundle of sticks. "You is my chirren," she said. "You my choir for sure. An' listen at me: Ain't no one stan' in front of you for goodness, no. You is the best, o' the best."

The Grace Notes were rapt with attention, for they believed her words, heart and soul.

"When you sing," Odessa continued, "look on down at the front row of peoples. They is always a empty chair there. See it?"

The children nodded. Yes, they saw it.

"Know who that chair for?"

They shook their heads, but they knew that they would know.

She said, "It's for me, Babies. I'm wiff you, yestiday, today, tomorrow, an' all the tomorrows after that. An' you know how I can say such a mackulous thing?" At this, Miz Preacher put a long arm into the air and said, "Because we be in Jesus, old-uns, an' young-uns, and me and you together. Jesus hold us in his hand, and ain't no one gonna snatch us out, never, not never."

Mary reached out and touched Odessa's hand. She had come to love the old woman. For this is the power of a wise love wisely expressed: to transfigure a heart suddenly and forever.

That was Sunday. On Tuesday, the twenty-second of December, Miz Odessa Williams turned her face to the wall and gave up the ghost.

Then the funeral preparations had to be done in a hurry because there were only two days in which to accomplish them.

Friday was out. That was Christmas Day. So were Saturday and Sunday because Gaines Funeral Home was always closed on weekends. Odessa would have to be buried on Thursday, though that was Christmas Eve.

On Thursday at eleven a.m., Miz Odessa's casket was set in front of the chancel, its lid open so that mourners could view her body one last time before it was closed, and her memorial service began.

The Grace Notes came and sat in the last pew on my right-hand side. Among them, of course, was my daughter Mary.

She stood, stepped into the aisle, and started walking forward to Miz Odessa's open casket.

I joined her.

Odessa's eyelashes looked as if they were black threads that had stitched the lids together. The mortician had smeared her mouth with a fire-red lipstick, though she'd thought that any sort of makeup was garish, "Like one o' them breast-naked pole-swingin' womens that men pays paper money to be gawking at."

Compulsively, Mary reached out and touched the back of the dead woman's hand—then snatched it back, shivered, and said, "So cold! So cold."

I would have put my arm around her, but the child turned and marched—stomped—back to her friends in their pew.

My daughter had encountered death and had learned that there were ends to living things. Rare and precious things. Things that someone has come to love. Miz Odessa Williams, that fierce old lady. She too had an end. Was gone. Was dead.

While I stood in the aisle, preaching ("Now there shall be no gloom for her who was in anguish."), I noticed the expressions on the faces of the Grace Notes: grim, bordering on anger, and grown old because their deepest questions had no answers. They could not allow themselves, even unconsciously, to be angry at the great Almighty. I don't think they even knew *where* to aim their anger.

Something had to change their unhappy attitude.

But it could not be by rational explanations. Rationality is a reality, and reality can only make a bad mood worse. And they would be antagonized if someone should say, "Snap out of it!"

I didn't want to make light of the children's feelings. I wanted, rather, to give them an object to be angry at—the ability to say, "I *hate* you, Mister Death!"

It had to be a story.

Bruno Bettelheim writes,

> "True" stories about the "real" world may provide some interesting and often useful information. . . . But strictly

realistic stories run counter to the child's inner experiences; he will listen to them and maybe get something out of them, but he cannot extract much personal meaning from them that transcends obvious content. These stories inform without enriching. . . . But a fare of realistic stories only is barren.[1]

When children experience a story, it can, as I've said, shift their emotions from what is cruel to what is consoling. Fairy tales don't shy away from evil beings. Neither do the children shy away from wicked witches or trolls that live under bridges, a tale's monsters, because they trust that their pastors will end the story with salvation.

And so it was on the following Sunday morning that I said to the congregation that I had a story to tell the children but that the adults could listen to it too. What works for children works also for adults.

The sun is a living character in the story I entitled "Lily." For Lily, the sun is not an "it." He is a "he" because he is conscious of the life he lives and of his thinking, his talking, and his very being. He is a character capable of loving a child.

Like child, like adult. Consider Jotham's parable (Judg 9), in which the trees are personified, are metaphors for the people of our congregations. That parable is a story. "Lily" is a story.

In his book *The Child's Conception of the World*, Jean Piaget offers this insight—that a child attributes consciousness to things that "move of their own accord, like the sun or a bicycle."[2] He asks a child about the intelligence of things: "Is the moon intelligent?" And the child answers, "Yes, because it shines at night. It lights the streets and hunters in the forest too, I think."[3]

It is the same with the sun that lights the day. Children never question whether the sun lives or whether he can be a friend of theirs, for it does and it can.

Even so do the children of my congregation live within my story, *becoming* Lily and yearning to know whether the sun (like Jesus, the Son of God) can finally love them too.

Piaget asks a boy named Vern, "Is the heat of the sun natural?"

Vern answers yes in such a manner that Piaget explains, "For Vern, the heat of the sun is 'natural' since the sun is guided by an internal force towards an end that is useful to life." He follows that thought with this: "[The sun acts] by *moral* obligation—not to do things it ought not to do."[4]

With these axioms in mind, we turn to the story in my Sunday-morning sermon.

Once upon a time, three sisters lived at the southern edge of the northernmost forest in all the land, a place where the sun shines for most of the summer and sleeps for most of the winter, when the moon and the stars cast a pale light on the earth.

The sisters were plants with roots that reached deep in a rich soil.

Sister Bean, the oldest of the three, was a plain sort of plant but a very good worker. She said, "I'm better than my sisters," because she was always busy catching the sun's bright rays in her catcher's glove of green leaves, then skillfully turning the sun's rays into sugar.

In June, Sister Bean's flowers were little white and homely purses. By the end of July, they had become long, dry pods hanging from her arms, and she called all comers to come and eat. "I am," she boasted, "the most important person in the land!"

In the month of August, Sister Marigold put on the crown of a princess. Her petals were so golden and glorious that she said, "I am a knockout! Just look at me. I outshine the sun itself."

The beautiful Sister Marigold and the busy Sister Bean had many friends. They invited them to come to their parties, to feast on good food, to dance, and to listen to Sister Marigold's tuneful songs:

Love is soft, love is sweet,
Love is good speech
(Tee-hee).

As for Sister Lily, her two older sisters mocked her. They said to their guests, "Ignore her. She's a dreamer. She talks to *things* and pretends that they answer her."

Sister Marigold jeered, "I'm a beauty. You are ugly—one skinny stem with little unpretty and flippity leaves."

Sister Bean said, "You don't work. Lazy and loafing all the day long."

What Sister Lily did, she talked to Sun. When he rose at dawn, he smiled and said, "Good," and Sister Lily answered, "Morning." They said, "Good morning," and that's how they talked together.

Sister Bean said, "The sun doesn't talk."

Sister Lily said, "Maybe not. Maybe so."

"What the sun does," said Sister Bean, "is it beams on my leaves, making sugar, and *that's* why it's here."

At noontime, Sun said, "Good," and Sister Lily answered, "Day." They said, "Good day," and that's how they talked together.

Sister Marigold said, "The sun doesn't talk."

Sister Lily said, "Maybe not. Maybe so."

In the evening, Sun sat on the rim of the western horizon, tired and ready to sleep. He said, "Good," but Sister Lily never answered, "Bye." Such a terrible word, that *goodbye*, because it might mean the two people will never meet again. Sister Lily had started to love Sun, and she longed to know if Sun might one day love her too.

Sister Bean was very vain. In the month of October, she said, "I have done my duty so well and so righteously that I have proved myself to be the most important worker in all the land."

At the same time, Sister Marigold's princess crown was at its goldenest. "Beauty," she said, "will get a good reward."

By November, the weather had turned very cold, and the wind had a stinging bite.

The trees dressed in their finery of fiery colors, and the animals and the birds began to talk about going south.

Finally, the trees lost all their leaves, and all the growing things withered, and the squirrels had squirreled their acorns underground, and the mice had stored their grass seeds in their tunnels, and the swans got ready to fly south, and now the sisters worried about being left all alone.

The animals said, "Beware! The killer is coming. And he kills by kissing!"

The squirrels hurried into their nests, and the mice burrowed underground, and the swans spread their white and graceful wings and sailed to warmer climes.

Sister Bean and Sister Marigold heard a sniffling and a sobbing and then a downright boo-hooing, and they asked, "What now, Sister Lily?"

And she said, "Sun is dying."

Both of her sisters yelled, "The sun is a fire! Fire and light are not alive. They *can't* die!"

Sister Lily whispered, "But look how late he gets up in the morning, and how weak he is when he travels the sky, and how early he goes to bed at night." And she wept, "He never told me that he loves me."

Indeed, the sisters agreed that day by diminishing day, the sun was descending into darkness.

But Sister Bean harrumphed, "I've made food to last long, however cold it gets."

Haughty Sister Marigold said, "When the sun is snuffed, I will be the sun that lights the land."

By January, Sister Bean could not stop shivering, and Sister Marigold's golden petals turned brown and withered and fell.

Now it was Sister Lily who heard a sniffling and a sobbing and a downright boo-hooing.

"Wait!" she called. "Wait! Just before he went down under the earth, Sun said one last word. He said, 'Again!'"

Then here came the killer, colder than the Frost Giant!

Sister Bean screamed, "Not fair! I've been a righteous worker! I don't deserve to die!"

Sister Lily said, "But Sun said, 'Again!'"

Sister Marigold screamed, "Not fair! I've shed my golden glory on the land, and not a penny in return! I don't deserve to die!"

Sister Lily said, "But Sun said, 'Again!'"

At this point, I stopped my story and asked the children, "What do you think that killer is?"

They cried out, "Winter!"

The children knew. They understood—and then I went on with my story.

The winter wind kissed Sister Bean with its freezing and deadly kiss, and then she was left standing on one leg in a snowy field, quivering in the wind because she was dead.

Sister Marigold tried to hide by pushing her head underground. But winter freezes everything, even the earth. It kissed her with its killing kiss, and then the whole earth was silent except for the hissing of the wind through the naked branches.

No, there *was* one other sound. Sister Lily was crying out, "I hate you! I *hate* you, Mister Death, because you took my sisters away from me!"

And there it was—what I hoped to happen happened. The children had found a thing to be angry at: "I hate you, Mister Winter!"

But every child and every Grace Note felt sad because Sister Lily had also died.

So now I had to finish my Lily story with salvation.

I said, "But winter doesn't last forever. I'll tell you what I'll do. When Easter comes around, I'll lead you to the southern edge of the northernmost forest, and we will see there a pure white blossom, and you will look inside of it, and you will ask, 'That's a dewdrop, right?'"

And I will say, "No, that's a tear of joy, a pearl of great price, for Sun has kissed Sister Lily, and *his* kiss is not the killer's kiss. His kiss is a kiss of life and love."

Finally, I ended off my sermon by saying to the congregation, "And what does all this mean? It means that God has kissed us all with his grace and his mercy and his loving-kindness."

Thus my (fairy) tale granted my listeners a passage from grieving to loving.

The best of our story-sermons can become our congregations' genuine experience. A member of the congregation might recall it long after hearing it and then can tell it over again to other people.

Just so did Mary Ellen Philips tell "Lily" to her sixteen-year-old niece Rachel.

Several years earlier, Rachel's legs had suffered a crippling disease, which confined her to a wheelchair. At the same time, she had a boyfriend, Robert, who was a quadriplegic. The two of them communicated by telephone and letters and cards.

The narrow sidewalk in Robert's backyard descended on a gentle, barely visible slope away from his house. One day his mother pushed him out onto that sidewalk to enjoy the sunshine and the sweet spring breezes. She locked the chair's wheels and left him there, facing away from the house.

But she hadn't locked the wheels properly.

It wasn't long before the chair began to roll slowly forward and down the sidewalk. It gathered speed until one of its wheels slipped off the edge and hit a bump, causing the chair to fall over on its side. One of its aluminum armrests pressed on Robert's throat and cut off his breath. Robert suffocated and died.

Mary Ellen received a telephone call from her sister, Rachel's mother.

"Oh, Mary! Rachel's friend Robert was buried last week. She won't eat. She can't sleep. She won't even talk to me. Pastor Johnson tried to console her, but it did no good, and I am at my wit's end."

Mary Ellen was a painter of simple things. She set up a small easel in Rachel's bedroom and painted a moon and stars in a dark sky while she sang,

> *Sleep, baby, sleep.*
> *The large stars are the sheep,*
> *The little stars are the lambs,*
> *The gentle moon is the shepherdess.*
> *Sleep, baby, sleep.*

The next morning, Rachel asked for a drink of water. It was a good beginning! Her mother hurried to the kitchen and came back with a glass of water. She scrambled an egg. She toasted two slices of bread. She brought the food with a glass of orange juice to her daughter. But Rachel refused to eat. Her face was blotched with emotion, and she had set her teeth against the spiteful world.

That same evening, Mary Ellen sat down on the side of Rachel's bed and said, "What can I do for you?"

Rachel spoke almost as if it were a demand: "Tell me 'Lily.'"

Mary did. She told her niece the story from its beginning to its end.

Rachel said, "Tell it again."

The next morning, she asked to be told the story yet again.

When Mary Ellen had ended by saying, "His kiss is a kiss of life and love," Rachel started to sob and sob.

She had made the transition. She *was* Sister Lily and had been set free.

Mary Ellen allowed her niece to cry and cry.

*Remember, the
entrance door to the sanctuary is
inside you. . . .*

*Each of us
has a secret companion musician to
dance to.*[5]

3

What Does Faith Have to Do with It?

Now, faith in this case is composed of the axioms by which every person makes sense of a world that is otherwise absurd. Faith is the root that blossoms, albeit unconsciously, into our intelligible and world-interpreting stories.

It doesn't matter *whose* faith it is, whether Christian or Jewish or Muslim or juju or agnostic or the rituals of the ancient Greeks.

A well-told story reveals what has been hidden, sub specie aeternitatis, within our and our congregations' deepest selves. It gives our people eyes that see and ears that hear and tongues that taste and fingers that touch and hearts that can be moved, thereby turning their daily realities into images that can be experienced.

And even before we start to create a story, and then to tell it, we should trust that we have the ability to craft it well enough to lead our listeners to the truth.

Someone might ask us, "What will your story say?" But it's better to ask, "What will your story *do*?" Rainer Maria Rilke might answer with this poem:

> Tell us, poet, what it is you do.
> —I praise.

> But in the midst of deadly turmoil, what
> helps you endure, and how do you survive?
> 	—I praise.
> And that which nameless is, anonymous,
> how do you, poet, still call out to them?
> 	—I praise.
> Who grants your right to pose in any guise,
> wear any mask, and still remain sincere?
> 	—I praise.
> And that the stillness and the violence,
> like star and storm—know and acknowledge you?
> 	—because I praise.[1]

Martin Buber, in his book *I and Thou*, explains what sorts of relationships might be established among the "I" of a person, and created nature, and other people, and the Eternal. Let storytelling preachers be the "I" in Buber's imagistic philosophy. He writes,

> The world is twofold for an individual in accordance with his twofold attitude. The attitude of man is twofold in accordance with the two basic words he can speak. The basic words are not single but word-pairs. One basic word is the word pair "I-You." The other basic word is the word pair "I-It." But this basic word is not changed when He or She takes the place of "It." . . . But the "I" of the basic word "I-You" is different from that in the basic word "I-It."

Regarding the qualities of our story-preaching relationships, he writes,

> Basic words do not state something that might exist outside them; by being spoken they establish a mode of existence. Basic words are spoken with one's [my, your] being.

When one says, "You," the "I" of the word pair "I-You" is said, too. When one says, "I" of the word pair "I-It" is said too. . . . The basic word of the word "I-You" can only be spoken with one's whole being. The basic word "I-It" can never be spoken with one's whole being. . . . Whoever speaks one of the basic words enters into the word and stands in it.[2]

Keep thinking, keep pondering on Buber's exposition, and we might be able to find ourselves inside his complexities—how we can preach a story with our whole beings—a truly wonderful experience.

4

Right Ways and Wrong Ways to Tell a Children's Story

After I'd published *The Book of the Dun Cow* in 1978, Maurice Sendak telephoned me and asked how old I was.

"Thirty-five," I said.

Then he said that he was glad that I was young because I had not yet been driven to cynicism. He said that he hoped I'd be resilient enough to survive the inalterable administrations of publishers with my spirit intact. After that, he became something like an elder companion to a younger writer. He had already gone the rugged road of sanctimonious criticism.

Where the Wild Things Are was published in 1963 without much fanfare. But it wasn't long before it became known because of the criticisms from parents and professionals alike. It was, they said, a frightening book. Educators and librarians and guardians of children's innocence said that the story and its pictures would trouble the small children, would even harm them psychologically, and would surely give them nightmares.

One librarian wrote that *Where the Wild Things Are* was the sort of book that a child might come upon in the dark of the day.

Sleep? Sendak hath murdered sleep.

They were wrong, of course. The tenderhearted parent and the hyperbolic critic were wrong, and the book prevailed because, as Sendak said, it was true and altogether right.

Bettelheim again: "In reply to the question whether the fairy story tells the truth, the answer should address itself not to the issue of truth in factual terms, but to the child's concern of the moment."[1]

One of the most important commandments for the creation and the telling of a children's tale is this: thou shalt not condescend!

When a pastor or another member of the church sits down—say, in the chancel—during a worship service to chat with the children, they may often talk in a patronizing voice. But it is always better to speak as if they and the children are equals.

Adults who write to their *images* of what a child is, rather than writing out of their own experiential memories of their childhoods, do, in a real sense, talk baby talk. They make the conventional assumption that children are pastel-colored innocents—that they have an angelic goodness and that they are unsullied souls.

Consequently, the adults reduce the story to the taste of a sugar cookie. That attitude is offensive. Even as they presume to know things better than a child knows, they present themselves as tellers of tales far too simple and less knowledgeable than what children know. Simpletons tell simplistic stories.

Selma G. Lanes, in her book *Down the Rabbit Hole*, speaks about the futile effects of such stories:

> When . . . a grown person chooses a book for a young child, the act is often freighted with odd bits of . . . heavy and nebulous luggage: the unspoken responsibility not to sully that living possibility for perfection reborn with each new being. The weight of our future hopes as well as our

past regrets is the invisible burden that young children's books are always [forced to] bear.

On the other hand, to be a parent or any grownup in the real world who works at close range with children is to be constantly made aware of one's shortcomings in dealing with these flesh-and-blood possibilities for perfection. In how many trying situations are we shocked to find ourselves responding exactly as an erring mother or insensitive teacher once did to us. . . . One of the many little-acknowledged joys of young children's books is that they allow us, adult and child, momentarily to escape from failures and inadequacies . . . into a more tranquil world where any problem posed has a satisfactory answer.[2]

Note: children *and* adults. We, too, long to be released.

Sendak demonstrated over and over (witness his picture books *In the Night Kitchen* and *Outside over There*) that by his stories, boys and girls are moved through all this world's dangers to happy conclusions.

In his acceptance speech for the Caldecott Medal in 1964, Sendak explained to the assembled notorieties that fantasy was the best way to grant a child her catharsis.

Jesus told stories wherein his listeners lived as characters. His parables did not often end as many tales do, with "and they lived happily ever after." A story's evil remained an evil.

One story regards a man who owned a rich vineyard.[3] He leased it to tenants who would be paid a portion of its produce, then traveled away to a far country. When the season of the harvest came around, he sent a slave to the tenants, asking them for his share of the grapes.

But they beat that slave, and he returned to his master empty-handed.

He sent a second slave, whom the tenants also insulted and bruised with a harsher beating. He went back also empty-handed.

So the landowner said to himself, "I'll send them my only begotten son. Surely they will respect *him*."

But when the tenants saw him coming, they said, "This is the heir! Let's kill him, and the entire inheritance will be ours."

And that's what they did. They threw him out of the vineyard and killed him.

"What then," Jesus asked, "should the man do to the tenants? He destroyed them and gave his vineyard to others."

When he had finished his tale, his listeners said, "God forbid!"

But he fixed his eyes on the scribes and the Pharisees among the crowd and said, "What does my story mean?" He answered his own question, saying, "Have you never heard what the psalmist said? 'The stone that the builders rejected has become the chief cornerstone?' Everyone who falls on that stone will be broken into pieces, and it will crush anyone on whom it falls."

Those who dwell in a well-told story look around: its weather is their weather, its people's actions are their actions, its dialogue is theirs, and they are its characters.

It was the same with the scribes and Pharisees. They ground their teeth, for they perceived that Jesus was speaking about *them*. And he had told his parable with such an invasive skill that his enemies would have beaten him right then and there. But they restrained themselves because they feared that the crowd surrounding them might beat them first.

5

Naming I

Allow me an excursus, now, to discuss how a story's naming of things causes a radical transformation in those things.

In Hebrew, the name Jacob, Ya'aqob, is connected to the noun *'aqeb* (heel), referring, of course, to the fact that in the Bible, Jacob emerged from Rebekah's womb clutching the heel of his brother, Esau. Also, for obvious reasons, it is connected to the verb *'aqab* (to cheat), for he swindled his brother out of his heritage and usurped their father's blessing.

As this part of the story begins, it has been twenty years since Jacob's brother swore to kill him.[1] As Jacob returns to the land of his birth, he still fears Esau's wrath so much that he will not meet his brother face-to-face. Instead, he halts at the dry Jabbok wadi at the eastern shore of the Jordan River. In an effort to appease his brother, Jacob divides his cattle—goats, ewes, rams, milk camels, cows, bulls, and donkeys—and servants and rich possessions, sending these divisions one after the other across the Jordan. Finally, he sends his large family across and then is left in the dark night alone.

No, not altogether alone. A night spirit comes and wrestles with him—a titanic wrestling match, for the Israelites remembered their patriarchs as powerful and great of stature. Witness Jacob's strength to raise the stone he'd slept on into a ponderously heavy, enduring, and immoveable monument.

When day begins to break, Jacob says, "Tell me your name."

Ancient eastern peoples believed that to know and to speak the name of a powerful, numinous spirit was to take control of it.

Rather than speaking its name, the night spirit asks for Jacob's name.

Jacob answers, "Jacob."

The spirit says, "You shall no longer be called 'Jacob,' but you shall be called 'Israel' because you have wrestled with God and with humanity and have prevailed."

"With God" can mean "against God." Or else it can mean "on God's side." In Jacob's case, both were true. When the spirit vanishes at dawn, Jacob has been radically transformed. The name Israel has effected the change in him.

It's the same with the name Simon bar Jonah. It refers to and it embraces all that this man has been since his father had named him Simon.

But when Jesus changes his name to Peter, the name also changes the man. He will be the rock upon which Jesus will "build my church, and the gates of hell shall not prevail against it" (Matt 16:18 ESV). On the other hand, his iniquities will shatter that rock to pieces, and on each piece will be written the names of his many sins.

Naming something makes it familiar in your life.

–NPR, 12:30, August 16, 2020

Individuals *are* their names.

Usually, we think of a name as the "handle" by which we indicate a person. "Walt" is like a sign that refers to a Walter, as in "we've invited Walt to the party." But when someone says, "Walt,

I'm so glad you came," the name is no longer a reference, a pointing to a someone over there. That "Walt" *is* Walt.

While driving east on Highway 30, I see a sign that says "10 miles to Valparaiso." Obviously, the sign is not the city. It is when I arrive in the city that "Valparaiso" is not a referential name. It *is* its name. Likewise, the name of a story can be more than just its title. The story whole is its name too.

It used to be (and still may be) the practice of the western Plains Indians that at thirteen or fourteen years old, girls and boys would be given names befitting their characters and their personal substances.

Again, the true name of a story is not its title. It is the story itself that, in the telling, names an experience that the listener has felt before but had neither known that she felt it nor understood its meaning—until a well-told story names it and thereby makes her aware of it.

We might forget a story's title, but because of its effect on us, we will surely remember the experience.

Joe Morgenstern reviews movies for the *Wall Street Journal*. Recently, he reviewed a film directed by Chloé Zhao, *Nomadland*, of which he wrote, "Stirring, profound, poignantly funny, and almost literally transporting, [this film] leaves you full of feelings you may not have known you had."[2]

6

Naming II

Without a doubt, you know that the Hebrew word *dabar* has two meanings: "word" and "deed." God's utterance is *itself* God's doing.

"In the beginning God created the heavens and the earth" (Gen 1:1 NKJV)—by speaking them into being.

The creating word, "light," *was* the word, and light's appearance was the act.

That divine word did not command the obedience of the light as though it were a separate entity. Nor did the Creator act like an engineer who designed and manufactured light. In that case, the speaker and the "light" would be divided, God the subject and light the object in the sentence of creation. Nor was "light" like a mane-flaming stallion galloping through the primeval night. God's cry "Light!" *was* light.

Thus God's language was the stark creation of things. Yet there was a second language. The naming: firmament, "sky"; dry land, "earth"; the gathered waters, "sea."

I recall that C. S. Lewis said something like this: if humans tried to speak God's first language, they would have created monsters. False and self-serving stories or poetry or novels can be spectral monsters in themselves.

The Creator also spoke a second language, which was given to humanity also to speak.

This language was naming.

"The man gave names to all cattle, and to the birds of the air, and to every animal of the field" (Gen 2:20), and "Whatever the man called every living creature, that was its name" (Gen 2:19).

More wonderfully, the names that humans give humans bring the unnamed ones into being, granting each their identities and their individual personhoods: "The man named his wife Eve, because she was the mother of all living" (Gen 3:20).

Both God's naming and our ability to name accomplish three separate revelations.

1. That which exists but which hasn't been named cannot be known. For the Hebrews, language is the stuff of knowing. When a created thing is named, it enters the realm of human awareness. To name it, then, is to clothe it in visibility. It appears.

2. That which has been named enters the grammar of existence. So Louis Dupré: "Words can do much more than, for instance, pictures, which represent an object by giving an arrangement of parts analogous to that of the depicted object. Words *name* relations and by doing so are able to embody concepts not only of things, but of things in combination."[1]

As words are joined to words in the structure of a sentence, so every named thing stands in a living relation—stands in a sweet kinship with every other named thing in the universe. And since one word will enjoy an infinite variety of grammatical relationships, things—particularly humans—will also enjoy a relationship with the community of other people.

3. Our relationship with the divine, our covenant with Christ, is established by our having been named. Moreover, our names declare our purpose: to serve the earth and its inhabitants, the populations of all its peoples.

"You are a chosen race, a royal priesthood" (1 Pet 2:9 ESV).

One of our purposes is to be God's priests: "Receive the Holy Spirit. If you forgive the sins of any, they are forgiven them; if you retain the *sins* of any, they are retained" (John 20:22-23 NKJV).

We are witnesses to, and preachers of, the gospel, the death and the resurrection and the grace of Christ Jesus, and there is no naming as significant as the naming by humans of humans.

Thus our first mother's name, Eve, conferred on her character, her very identity, and her purpose: to be the ancestress of the first generation, and the second, and all the generations that followed, even down to today.

It's well known that the Hebrew words *ishshah* and *ish* make the same pun in English: "wo-man" and "man." The short word, "man," is the root of the longer word, "woman." And that longer word, "woman," finds its fullness in "man."

They are equals because each one needs the other. Eve did not sin of her own accord, as the male-dominated church used to believe.

No. God said, "It is not good that the man [read 'anyone'] should be alone" (Gen 2:18).

If there was a fault, it was that Eve, *ishshah*, did what she did separate from Adam, *ish*.

Later in Genesis (25:24-26), Rebekah and Isaac named their two sons. Again, their names were not mere "handles"—names that only referred to the twins. Rather, they contained their characters.

I have already spoken about Jacob's name. Esau's name, too, characterized him at his birth, for he entered the world red, ruddy.

By their name—"the Children of Israel"—the Israelites awoke to a fresh knowledge of themselves and realized that it was by God's power that they escaped Egypt and that they were saved by the Lord's servant, Moses, his rod and his staff.

And the ritual of their salvation they named according to what it did and what it accomplished—Passover. They named it what it was: the Passover.

God had changed their relationship to Pharaoh, whose breath and spirit they watched bubbling on the surface of the sea.

Just as a name can be a person or a people, so can a story, by its narrative progression, find its own name.

Robert Frost writes, "For me the initial delight is in the surprise of remembering something I didn't know that I knew." And again, "It [a poem or a story that is not unlike a poem] finds its own name as it goes and discovers the best waiting for it in some final phrase at once wise and sad."[2]

In the same vein, William Stafford, in his book *Writing the Australian Crawl*, offers an example of how a poem learns its name not *before* it is written but *while* it is being written. Likewise, a congregation learns the name of an experience not by a title but by the story whole.

Stafford writes,

> One morning, doodling, trying to write before I could think, I put down, "The seed that met water. . . ." Of course, this kind of meeting is potential, in a small way, and my next move was to crawfish back from that potential, even while allowing it to exist, by saying that the seed that met water "spoke a little name." By this time I was in retreat, and I give you the poem, mostly just a little evasion, or excursion, then a payoff.[3]

Note how the poet does not know, at first, where the poem is going. It is leading *him*. And if he can't know that, he can't know its name until it is complete and has discovered *its* own name.

Stafford continues by inscribing his poem whole:

B. C.

The seed that met water spoke a little name.

(Great sunflowers were lording the air that day;
this was before Jesus, before Rome; that other air
was readying our hundreds of years to say things
that rain has beat down on over broken stones
and heaped behind us many slag lands.)

Quiet in the earth a drop of water came,
and the little seed spoke: "Sequoia is my name."[4]

Louis Ginzberg writes in his *The Legends of the Jews*, "As the name of a man clings to him, so men cling to names. For the primitive savage the name is part of the essence of a person or thing."[5]

Here ends my excursus.

PART II

To Build a Story

7

Composing a Story Step by Step

We tale-telling preachers can take a lesson from William Stafford's progressive method.

I'll use my story "Lily" as an example for the construction of *our* stories.

First, ask, "What is this story for? What should it *do?*"

Before I began to write "Lily," and even before I imagined my story, I wondered how I could change the Grace Notes' distress and how I could comfort them.

A story need not be told only to children. Parents too might be suffering some strong emotion. Or an adult member of the congregation might be confronted by some tribulation or be depressed or lonely. Another member might be grieving the death of someone she has loved.

What follows are the five steps I take to develop stories like "Lily."

I suggest that preachers generally might use these steps to create their own stories.

Create Similar yet Dissimilar Characters

Create characters who are like the characters who will appear in the story and yet unlike them in that they are metaphors. I created the character named Sister Lily with whom children could identify because she, as I conceived her, had the same feelings, the same yearnings, and the same unhappiness that they, like Sister Lily, were experiencing. But she is also a metaphor. She is a flower. Hence she might grow into a goodness and take the children along with her. And the sun is a metaphor for Jesus.

In that same manner, I personified Sister Lily's sisters, and the animals, and the winter that kills by kissing. Winter *was* death. ("I hate you, Mister Death!")

In order to increase the metaphoric reality, I placed my characters into a visible setting. Hence Sister Bean and Sister Marigold and Sister Lily live at the edge of the northernmost forest in the world. The setting doesn't have to be any more detailed than that.

Nor did I want to make my characters mere abstractions. They had to be seen and heard and almost touchable, and I distinguished them with only a detail or two: how they act, how they talk, and their differing moods.

Sister Bean is proud of her work—the self-righteous sister.

Sister Marigold is proud of her beauty—the haughty sister.

But Sister Lily has no pride at all. She's humble, unselfconscious, uncomely, and altogether blameless—loving and hoping to be loved.

If the story is well told and persuasive, it becomes the house in which a child is living.

Be Aware of the Pattern You Are Creating

A good story has a pattern. When we begin with something that catches our hearers' interest right from the start, they will want to *keep* listening to find out what's going to happen next.

Hans Christian Andersen starts his tale "The Little Match Girl" with this hook:

It was dreadfully cold, and turning dark. It was the last evening of the year, New Year's Eve. In this cold and darkness walked a little girl. She was poor and both her head and her feet were bare. Oh, she had a pair of slippers when she left home; but they had been too big for her—in truth they belonged to her mother. The little one had lost them while hurrying across the street to get out of the way of two carriages.[1]

Likewise, the first verse (the first four lines) of James Weldon Johnson's "The Creation" is not unlike a sermon. In fact, his poem is the whole of his sermon without interruptions or explanations or commentary. He himself asserts that he is preaching a sermon. Witness the subtitle of his *God's Trombones: Seven Negro Sermons in Verse.*

Who, having heard Johnson's voice and his imagery, would *not* be captivated?

And God stepped out on space,
And he looked around and said:
I'm lonely—
I'll make me a world.[2]

The words of the first chapter in Herbert Anderson and Edward Foley's book *Mighty Stories, Dangerous Rituals* are these: "In the aftermath of the massacres that occurred in Rwanda in the early 1990s, a woman psychologist was asked to visit one of the many refugee camps of Rwandans in Tanzania."[3]

Stay Open to a Clarity of Purpose

Going forward, the story itself might lead its author to an understanding and a clarification of its actual purpose. My "Lily" tale was to help children confront malice and mortality with such bravery that they can battle through these tribulations unto victory.

Let's say that a purpose is to diminish a (sometimes scandalous) pride, not by open accusations (sinners in the hands of an angry God and so forth), but by a companionable and directing story like Frank Baum's *The Wonderful Wizard of Oz* or like Jesus's parable about the one lamb lost.

In the fourth chapter of his first letter to the Thessalonians, Saint Paul's purpose is to comfort those who fear for their friends who have already died. Though the apostle's persuasions are not written in the form of a story, their context *is* a story—he sends them an epistle written in the ink of affection. We too can develop a story of our own, basing it on Paul's words of consolation to Thessalonica.

Paul writes,

> But we do not want you to be uninformed, brothers and sisters, about those who have died, so that you may not grieve as others do who have no hope. [*Note the distinction: we also grieve, but hope tempers our grief.*] For since we believe that Jesus died and rose again, even so, through Jesus, God will bring with him those who have died. (1 Thess 4:13-14)

And we: "A mother is the last to leave the graveside of her son. At first she is dry-eyed, then her tears fall silently down."

Actually, the NRSV translates "those who have died" for Paul's more accurate image: "those which are asleep."

Be Attentive to the Plotline of the Story

Eugene L. Lowry writes in *The Sermon*, "And the *story sermon's* plot—it all depends on the story, the preacher, and the purpose, but it won't end until the resolution happens. The key to the plotting of the plotting operation of the sermonic story is, of course, the inclusion of characters, setting, action, and tone—all working out the plot from opening disequilibrium to final resolution."[4]

The story's events should be told in its chronological sequence, each part increasing the tension and causing our listeners' hearts to beat a little faster, always hoping to experience a satisfying solution. Witness Sister Lily's conflict with her sisters, then her greater conflict with the winter that kills by kissing, and then her Easter resurrection.

Jesus's parable about the prodigal son increases the tension between the prodigal and his father, until he suffers the more menacing conflict between his soul and himself—a wretchedly lonely young man because he had severed himself from his father. This, he believes, is a sin that his father would not forgive.

But if we shuffle the story's chronological events willy-nilly, there will be no tension at all. The tale will have crumbled into a senseless mess that a listener cannot experience. It will have been twaddle, a mere babbling, and a bore.

And the plot should not hop from scene to scene but build each scene on the previous one. And we should weave the story's events—the characters' developing moods and their actions and the increasing conflicts between the characters (Sister Lily and Mister Death)—throughout the whole story.

Be Conscious of the Diction of Your Speech

Without giving it a second thought, most of us preach in our natural, common, and conversational diction. But we can choose to speak in two other dictions: an easy, streetwise speech and one more formal.

Flannery O'Connor's narrators speak in the natural language that is familiar to us all. But her characters speak in a rude and unsophisticated language. Listen to the diction from her story "The Life You Save May Be Your Own":

Narrator: That night, rocking on her porch, the old woman began her business, at once.

The old woman: "You want you an innocent woman, don't you?" And then, "You don't want none of this trash. One that can't talk, can't sass you back or use foul language."

For an example of formal language, I return to T. S. Eliot and a quote from his essay "Religion and Literature":

> It is our business as Christians, *as well as* readers of literature to know what we ought to like. It is our business as honest men not to assume that whatever we like is what we ought to like; and it is our business as honest Christians not to assume that what we do like what we ought to like. And the last thing I would wish for would be the existence of two literatures, one for Christian consumption and the other for the pagan world.[5]

I suggest that we ought to spend time reading such literature as C. S. Lewis's *Mere Christianity* or *The Great Divorce*; Charles Dickens's slim novel *Hard Times*; a good translation of Hans Christian Andersen's fairy tales; a well-written history book about, say, the Civil War; Abraham Lincoln's inaugural address; a good detective novel (Agatha Christie's *Murder on the Orient Express* and maybe Edgar Allan Poe); romance novels; poetry, if we are so inclined; an articulate magazine (*Field & Stream? Good Housekeeping?*); a well-written blog.

Some of us might think that such readings are an entertainment and a waste of time—that it would be better to be reading commentaries, exegetical books, pastoral counseling books. But T. S. Eliot writes, "It is assumed that the rest of our reading is for our amusement, merely killing time. But I incline to come to the alarming conclusion that it is just the literature that we read for 'amusement,' or purely for 'pleasure' that may have the greatest and less suspected influence upon us."[6]

It's a good practice to listen to the tones of our voices when preaching. Is our voice spoken in flat, emotionless tones? Do we have, as it were, a "pulpit tone"? Do we speak, say, the word *God* as we would never speak it in normal speech? "Gawd." Or do we string it out a little longer than usual? Dr. Walter Stuenkel, a roundish man ("Oh, Mother, my wife! My tunny is happy!") and the president of Concordia Junior College, Milwaukee—an institution that I in my youth attended—would always rise up on his toes and bounce, saying, "God," rotund, full throated, and loud.

Not every reader makes a leader. But every leader must be a reader.

—Harry S. Truman

8

Making Our Stories Feel Real

A mother has just finished reading a bedtime story to her children, a fairy tale with trolls or witches, giants or terrible beasts. To comfort them and to disabuse them of such fictions, she says, "Of course, witches aren't real."

But the children answer, "No, Mama; not real. The story is true."

Bruno Bettelheim again:

> [Children's] parents or teachers tell [them] that things cannot feel and act; and as much as they may pretend to believe this to please these adults, or not to be ridiculed, deep down the [children] know better. Subjected to the rational teachers of others, [children] only bury their true knowledge deeper in [their] souls, it remains untouched by rationality; but it can be formed and informed by what the tales have to say.[1]

One of the ways to give life to a tale is to base it on our own personal experiences, and if it is well told, it can profoundly change our listeners.

David H. C. Read preached a sermon entitled "Too Much Talk?," in which he told a story taken from his own experience:

One of my first impressions when returning home after five years in a prison camp was that everyone was taking, talking, talking about nothing in particular. We had, without realizing it, gradually eliminated all unnecessary chatter. We spoke only to communicate information, or when we deliberately wanted a discussion to pass the time. I see now that talk is a lubricant in a society where we don't know each other very well.[2]

When I was eight years old, I suffered a sad and hopeless loneliness. It was this experience that enabled me to give life to Sister Lily's loneliness. After I had become an adult, I wrote another story that was also true to one of my personal experiences.

The purpose of "Lily" had been to give a listening child the power to cry out her anger against death and then to rise to a newness of life. The purpose of *this* next story, "Potter," was to help children overcome the pain of a grievous death (of a parent or a sibling or a close friend) but in the end to be granted a visionary resurrection not unlike Christ's rising from his tomb.

I know some adults who believe that no child should be taken to a funeral and to look at someone whom they loved now lying in a casket. "It will give them nightmares," they say. But children grieve better and heal faster than adults do. Yet because of the adults' own painful and lingering grief, they believe that a child's severe distress must be more distressful and longer lived than theirs.

Likewise, people were disturbed by my "Potter," claiming that it should not be read to the sensitive souls of schoolchildren. A mother believes that she is protecting her daughter, when, in fact, she's withholding from the child the opportunity to learn how to confront the dying and death.

Potter was the protagonist of my story. Potter was me.

I was nine years old when I made friends with a kid who lived three houses down from my house. He had a Scotsman's red hair and a constellation of freckles. I gave him a name that wasn't his name: Jonathan Scanlan.

Those days, we were living in Grand Forks, North Dakota. The land beyond our backyard sloped gently down and then faster down and through a patch of woods to the Red River. Unlike almost all the rivers in the United States, this river flows north into Canada, draining into Lake Winnipeg. The spring thaw always melts the southern length of the body of this watery snake before its head melts in Canada. Consequently, the river bloats. It overwhelms its banks and floods the land.

On a bright, blue spring afternoon when a gentle breeze blew, scenting the air with the warm spring duff and a greening vegetation, Potter's friend Jonathan came skipping into his backyard carrying a sailboat built with a Tinkertoy mast and sails cut from a pillowcase.

"Hey, Potter!" he yelled up to Potter's bedroom window. "Look what I got! Dad made this for my birthday!"

Potter stuck his head out his window and called down, "Wow! A sail and everything!"

"Wanna try it out with me?"

But Potter had a croupy cough.

"I can't," he said. "Mom won't let me out of the house."

"Too bad, buddy. I'm going down to float my boat on the river. The sailor off to the sea! But I'll come back and tell you how it went."

But the Red River was at high flood stage.

Late that evening, Jonathan's dad telephoned Potter's dad: "Is my boy with you? He hasn't come home."

"Sorry, Malcom. No. He isn't here."

Malcom drew a sharp breath of panic and hung up.

That night, Potter stood at his window, watching as a dozen flashlight beams switched left and right on the waters. He was trying not to cry. Those beams looked like spears getting ready to pierce the side of the swollen snake and to kill it.

Potter heard the deep voices of men in the moonlight, shouting, "Jonathan! Jonathan Scanlan!"

Fathers went upriver in galoshes, beseeching the river's bank.

Potter kneeled at his window and watched all night long. He was scared. He couldn't sleep.

At daybreak, the men came slowly up the slope. Jonathan's father was carrying a boy across his arms and close to his breast. The boy's arms hung loosely down.

Then Potter overheard his father talking to his mother in the downstairs kitchen: "We found his body lying under shallow water. We didn't know why he hadn't just stood up and walked home. Or why the current hadn't carried his body away. Then we understood. A riverbed root had driven deeply up his nose and held him there."

Potter lay down belly flat on his bed, and covered his head with his pillow, and sobbed and sobbed. After there were no sobs left in him, he started to imagine his friend deep under the river water and wreathed in riverweed. His body was sea green. His mouth was open as if he had something to say, but mud clogged it. His eyes were open too, but they saw nothing. The eyes of the blind.

Oh, Jonathan!

Potter saw his friend's hair—a soft copper cloud with little fishes darting in and out. And there was that witch's choppy finger, sticking out of the riverbed and driven up into the nostril of Potter's best friend.

Oh, that hair! Oh, those freckles!

The second part of my story brings things round right. It is a fantasy. But a fantasy is nonetheless true. I wrote it as a resurrection.

Potter is taken to the far east, where the marvelous phoenix lives. That great bird is larger than an eagle and golden at the neck, with deep purple feathers; his tail is azure blue mixed with red roses, and he has a crest like a king's crown.

The young boy watches as that five-hundred-year-old bird bursts into flames and is consumed in the fire.

The boy feels every sad thing that he felt when Jonathan died.

But the next day, the phoenix rises out of his ashes, clean and new and fiercely beautiful.

Even so does Potter learn with gladness what happened to his dear friend, Jonathan.

Likewise, Johann Wolfgang von Goethe based his first novel, *The Sorrows of Young Werther*, on several experiences of his own.

He had developed an affection for an eighteen-year-old woman named Charlotte Buff. But she was affianced to a man named Johann Christian Kestner, with whom Goethe had, at first, been on friendly terms.

Goethe's infatuation for Charlotte increased until it became an embarrassment.

Kestner could not but help recognizing Goethe's fascination.

One evening when the three were at dinner together, Kestner suddenly rose up like an angry bear and yelled, "Never come back again!"

His belligerence crushed the hypersensitive Goethe, and the sting lasted a long time. This was the personal experience that he wove into *The Sorrows of Young Werther*.

Goethe was a man of fervid emotions, of unbounded enthusiasms, of an intense interest in the spirit, the depths, and the heights and the behaviors of humankind. Life was for the living.

He also constructed his novel on another man's experience. As Goethe himself had, the character named Karl Wilhelm Jerusalem conceived an illicit passion for the wife of a court official. But because it was not requited, he went out and put a bullet in his body.

Goethe's book had a profound effect on the young men who lived in that romantic age. The work of an artist, the experience of a profound writer, gave life to his novel.

Likewise, by an engaging and fascinating tale, we preachers, we storytellers, can reshape the characteristics of those who are listening and hanging on our words.

Goethe's *The Sorrows of Young Werther* did just that—except that his novel did not end well. Goethe lived in a time of extreme romanticism, and many a young man influenced deeply by his story committed suicide.

Immanuel Kant extols the spiritual effect that a story may have on those who hear it. It can stir up a soul to the most profound acts of love. In his *Observations on the Feeling of the Beautiful and Sublime*, he writes,

> In [the sublime] are portrayed magnificent sacrifices for another's welfare, bold, resolution in peril, and a proven loyalty. . . . Their love is sad, fond, and full of respect; the misfortune of others stirs feelings of sympathy in [the listener's] breast and causes his generous heart to beat for the distress of others.[3]

Sacrifice is the measure of a genuine love. It need not be different for us who preach a good story.

Julian of Norwich preserves her own personal experiences in her writings—writings as artful as the best literature in the fifteenth century. It never occurred to her that what she wrote might be printed in a book, nor that more than a few people would read it and be influenced by it. But a whole host of people did and do read it, enflaming their spirits with the deeper love for Christ Jesus. She writes,

> After this the lord browte to my mynd the longyng that I had to hym aforn; and I saw that nothing letted me but synne, and so I beheld generally in us al. And methowte if synne had not a ben, we should al a ben clene and like to our lord as he made us; and thus, in my foly, aforn this tyme often I wondrid whi by the fret forseyng wysdam of God the begynnyng of synne was not lettid; for than, thowte me, al shulde a be wele. This steryng was mikel forsakyn, and nevertheless morning and sorrow I made therefore without reason and discretion. But Jesus, that in this vision enformid me of all that me neydeth, anserid by the worde and seyde: "Sin is behovabil, but al shal be wel, and al shal be wel, and all manner of thing shall be wele."[4]

And always, when I read Julian's words out loud, my spirit, too, grows warm with love.

In his preface to *God's Trombones*, James Weldon Johnson writes of his experience when he heard the preaching of a Black, dramatic, full-throated, and compelling preacher. The congregation's emotions could not help but be charged by their pastor's force. Johnson writes,

> At last he arose. He was a dark-brown man, handsome in his gigantic proportions. He appeared to be a bit self-conscious. . . . He started to preach a formal sermon from a formal text. The congregation sat apathetic and dozing. [The preacher] sensed that he was losing his audience and his opportunity. Suddenly he closed the Bible, stepped out from behind the pulpit, and began to preach. He started intoning the old folk-sermon that begins with the creation of the world and ends with Judgment Day. He was at once a changed man, free, and at ease, and masterful. The change

in the congregation was instantaneous. An electric current ran through the crowd. It was in a moment alive and quivering and all the while the preacher held it in the palm of his hand. He was wonderful in the way he employed his conscious and unconscious art. He strode the pulpit up and down in what was actually a very rhythmic dance, and he brought into play the full gamut of his wonderful voice, a voice—what shall I say?—not of an organ or a trumpet, but rather of a trombone.[5]

9

Spiritual Preparation

Because the telling of a tale forms an intimate covenant between we who preach and those who listen, I believe that we are duty bound to speak in faith, always praying that the source of our truths shall be the spirit of the Lord Jesus Christ, the grace and the mercy vouchsafed to us by his death and his resurrection. So before I describe the different stories in the next part of the book, I remind us of the need to prepare spiritually for the holy labor ahead.

I think that it is a good practice to prepare ourselves for worship, for presiding over a worship service, and for our story preaching by first secluding ourselves in a private place and murmuring our personal prayers. Here are but a few examples of such prayers.

The following is a prayer prayed by Saint Augustine that is attributed to his mentor in the faith, Saint Ambrose of Milan:

> Lord, let me seek you by calling upon you. Let me believe in you, for you have been preached to us. Lord, my faith calls upon you, that faith which you have given to me, which you have breathed into me by the incarnation of your Son and through the ministry of your preacher.[1]

And this is Martin Luther's sacristy prayer:

> O Lord God, dear Father in heaven, I am indeed unworthy of the office and ministry in which I am to make known Your glory and to nurture and serve this congregation.
>
> But since you have appointed me to be a pastor and a teacher, and because the people are in need of the teachings and the instructions, be my helper and let your holy angels attend me.
>
> Then, if you are pleased to accomplish anything through me, to Your glory and not to mine or to the praise of men, grant me, out of Your pure grace and mercy, a right understanding of Your Word and that I may also diligently perform it.
>
> O Lord Jesus Christ, Son of the living God, shepherd and bishop of our souls, send your Holy Spirit that He may work with me to will and to do through Your divine strength according to Your good pleasure, Amen.[2]

And here is a wonderfully applicable prayer taken from Carmen Bernos De Gasztold's *The Creatures' Choir*:

The Parrot

Did you say something,
Lord?
Oh! I thought
You were speaking to me.
You are silent?
Are you afraid
I shall tell
Your secrets?
It's true

*I'm a little talkative
but, at times,
that is useful:
heads are thick,
slow to understand,
and have to be told things
again and again.
If You need me,
I am your servant,
one who never grows tired
repeating the same word
again and again,
which has its power:
I may grow tedious
but people listen
in spite of themselves;
and what is repeated, repeated,
stays in the memory.
When may I serve
Your infinite wisdom?
Think of it, Lord.*

Amen.[3]

PART III

Six Sorts of Stories

I sing no harme good sooth to any wight,
To Lord or foole, Cuckold, beggar or knight,
To peace-teaching Lawyer, Proctor, or brave
Reformed or reduced Captiane, Knave.

—John Donne, "A Tale of a Citizen and His Wife"

10

Stories of Illustration

The first part of this book explained the effects of a well-told story. The second part opened ways by which to construct our stories. In this third part, now, I intend to focus on the stories themselves. As we move chapter by chapter from one sort of story to the next, I will unfold their differing qualities and purposes.

This first sort of story tends to be the most common one that we preachers tell. Stories that illustrate engage the intellect more than the emotion. They are similes: "This is like that. This story will help you *understand* the theme of my sermon." But if a story is *only* cerebral, a congregation cannot live inside of it—will not be able to experience it.

Most often, the illustrative story is told at the bang-beginning of the sermon.

Jesus introduced one of his illustrative stories with a simile: "The kingdom of heaven may be *compared* to a king who gave a wedding banquet for his son" (Matt 22:2; italics mine).

In 1 Corinthians 12, Saint Paul might have been joking (who knows?) when he compared the members of the Corinthian church to the human body, which cannot be separated into parts and still be alive.

The people in the house churches of Corinth had been squabbling about this and that, including who was baptized by whom and so forth. Hence *Paul's* comparison ("This is like that").

"If the whole body were an eye, where would the hearing be? If the whole body were an ear, where would be the sense of smell? [A joke.] But . . . it was God who arranged the members in the body according to his own choice."

The apostle continues by saying, "If all were a single [separated] member, where would the body be?" (1 Cor 12:19).

Here comes an eyeball rolling up the aisle. And there is a hand, finger walking up the same aisle, and the eyeball says to the hand, "I have no need of you."

Over there is a head sitting on its neck in the front pew, saying to the feet on the floor, "I have no need of you" (1 Cor 12:21).

Now the apostle's tone turns serious. He says,

> On the contrary, the members of the body that seem to be weaker are indispensable, and those members of the body that we think less honorable we clothe with greater honor, and our less respectable members are treated with greater respect. . . . But God has so arranged the body, giving the greater honor to the inferior member, that there may be no dissension within the body. (1 Cor 12:22-25)

Well, even though we can't preach like Paul, we can develop similes like his.

Several years ago, on the tenth Sunday after Pentecost, my wife and I visited a small church in Minnesota where we heard a truly wonderful sermon preached by a Black female preacher. When she stepped out of the pulpit, it was apparent that this pastor was monumentally pregnant.

The Gospel lesson appointed for that day was Matthew 13:45-46: "The kingdom of heaven is like a merchant in search of fine pearls; on finding one pearl of great value, he went and sold all that he had and bought it."

I had no doubt about how she would develop her simile.

The babe in her womb was, yes, that pearl. After she had delivered it, she would take a three-month leave of absence. She raised her fingers one by one, counting the prices she would have to pay.

"Give up the pleasures and the troubles of you whom I love. Forego preaching and, for a while, the ministry that defines me. I'll pay with sleepless nights. Visitors will overstock my kitchen with more casseroles than an army can eat. And what about my baby-birthing weight? Ah, me, no cakes or cookies or candy. No bacon. Dry toast with no jelly."

With a laugh, then, she told us that her greatest payment would be the loss of her shapely breasts: "They gonna grow as big as a shout."

A good and winsome and proper theologian, this pastor-preacher furthered her simile by explaining that that pearl of great price was Jesus Christ and his sacrificial death and the grace of his resurrection.

On the other hand, in another church in another state, my wife and I heard another preacher start his sermon with an illustration taken, appropriately, from a personal experience. But his illustration was not effective because of its lack of manner and its purpose.

He told the congregation that his father had been a farmer. When, he said, he was a boy of ten or eleven years old, he jumped out of his father's haymow and landed butt-first on a rat ("Ha, ha, ha!") and killed that rat "dead as a doornail. Ha!"

It was obvious to me that the purpose of his experience was to be a slaphappy and funny introduction, just as a comedian starts to engage his audience with a joke: "Well, friends. Aren't we all happy to be here?"

I remember the story well enough but not the rest of the sermon. He never again referred to his illustration. It was as detached as a head beheaded and quite dead upon delivery.

It *is* a good choice to begin a sermon with an illustration. And it will remain good so long as it is interwoven throughout the sermon.

In one of the sermons preached by Dr. Fred Niedner, he made reference to the fourth commandment: "Honor your father and your mother . . . so that it may go well with you in the land that the Lord your God is giving you."

Niedner likewise began his sermon with an illustration, a rather complicated one taken from Virgil's *Aeneid*. (He was, after all, an assiduous reader of good literature.)

His story was longer and more convoluted than most of us are able to tell. But I offer it here as an example of some lesser thing that we can construct.

Aeneas wants to leave the people of Troy and to travel home with his family. But his old, disabled father, Anchises, refuses to go. Anchises says that he'd rather die than face exile, until they see a bright star streaking across the night sky. An omen! They would imperil themselves if they disobeyed the sign.

Aeneas carried his aged father on his back.

After he'd told this story, Niedner explained that the Hebrew word for "honor" relates to the word *heaviness*. To honor one's parents does not mean to obey them—a mistaken rendering, perhaps, to give parents the right to demand their children's obedience.

Actually, it means that adult sons or daughters *carry* their parents.

Niedner, then, bases another story on his own personal experience.

While his father was dying and lying insensible on his bed, Niedner and his mother and his siblings sang hymns. This too was honoring their father, for they were bearing the man's spirit up to the stately mansions in heaven.

Saint Paul says, "Honor your father and your mother. This is the first commandment with a promise: that it will be 'well' (good! Glad!) with you, and you may live long on the earth."

Good: "And God saw that all he had made was very good."

Regarding all the stories that I will describe in the following chapters, there are many ways to fit them into a sermon.

One place is at the beginning, of course. Or we might tell them part by part throughout the sermon. The first part might be told at the sermon's beginning, after which preachers may preach a portion of that sermon's theme. Then we can return to the story's next part, say, in the middle of the sermon followed by a further explanation of its theme. And finally, we can conclude the sermon with the last part of our story.

11

Stories about the Presence and the Work of a Transforming God

These second kinds of stories cannot be fictitious, something we've made up. Rather, they should be actual personal experiences told faithfully and spiritually, always alert to the Holy Spirit's influence and the effects of her transforming presence. Here are six examples:

David Seeks God's Blessing

In Psalm 28, a "David" seeks and receives God's ear and the blessing of the Lord:

> To you, O Lord, I call; my rock, do not refuse to hear me, for if you are silent to me, I shall be like those who go down to the Pit. Hear the voice of my supplication, as I cry to you for help, as I lift up my hands toward your most holy sanctuary. (Ps 28:1–2)

Before was the prayer. Now is the psalmist's knowledge that he has been transformed by the God upon whom he had called:

> Blessed be the Lord, for he has heard the sound of my pleadings. The Lord is my strength and my shield; in him my heart trusts; so I am helped, and my heart exults, and with my song I give thanks to him. (Ps 28:6-7)

How good are the prayers of our own believing when we too are heard and transformed by the grace of the Lord Jesus Christ?

George Herbert's "Easter Wings"

The first two verses of George Herbert's "Easter Wings" are much like David's song in the Twenty-Eighth Psalm. Herbert does not doubt the omnipresence of the Lord and that he too has been transformed. Thus his poem adroitly recounts his spiritual transformation—his turnabout from falling to rising.

> *Lord, who createdst man in wealth and store*
> *Though foolishly he lost the same,*
> *Decaying more and more*
> *Till he became*
> *Most poor:*
> *With thee*
> *O let me rise*
> *As larks, harmoniously,*
> *And sing this day thy victories:*
> *Then shall the fall further the flight in me.*

> *My tender age in sorrow did begin:*
> *And still with sicknesses and shame*
> *Thou didst so punish sin,*
> *That I became*
> *Most thin.*
> *With thee*
> *Let me combine,*
> *And feel this day thy victory:*
> *For, if I imp my wing on thine,*
> *Affliction shall advance the flight in me.*

Stories of Old

The old stories are those once told—and maybe still are told—by desert nomads as they sat in a cold, nighttime darkness, warming themselves by flame-wavering fires—nomads telling again the magical tales of their ancestors.

There were heroes in those days: Mighty warriors born of Ishmael. Prophets infused with the words of God and who envisioned the faraway future. Men and women who had received the Lord's penetrating wisdom, wisdom that was passed down from age to age.

How wonderful were their ancestors! They were the first to tame wild camels and the first to trace the best passageways through the dead desert and to show the oases on the way. The first to sew tents of tanned goatskins.

Likewise, in the European Middle Ages, common folk and monks and nuns told stories about the saints who suffered torture and terrible martyrdom tranquilly because they knew that death was the door into the pure and peaceful and eternal kingdom of heaven. Here, then, is one of those saints' tales:

Saint Cecilia lived in the fifth century. Her mother was a Christian who raised her daughter to love and to model herself on the life of Christ.

Her father, on the other hand, was a grim Roman patrician with little love for anything else than his rank, his wealth, and his reputation. It provoked him that his only child wore coarse garments under her rich robe and that she gave *his* money to the poor. And it vexed him when he learned that his daughter in her thirteenth year had committed herself to Jesus Christ, to remain a virgin, and in spirit, to marry none other than the Holy Bridegroom.

Straightway, he went to another patrician and struck a business deal with him. He promised to pay the man a handsome bride-price if he would command his son Valerian to marry Cecilia.

What the fathers arrange the children must obey.

Valerian and Cecilia were married.

During their first night together, before they'd consummated their marriage, Cecilia whispered a secret to her new husband. "An angel of God watches over me," she said, "and I am afraid for you because if you touch me tonight, the angel will cause you to suffer torments. But if you honor my virginity, he will love you just as he loves me."

Now came God's transforming hand. Valerian was converted and was baptized as a Christian.

And again, God transformed many a Roman. Cecilia's winsome personality convinced them to turn away from their pagan gods and to venerate the One True and Triune God.

But the growth of the Christian community enraged a Roman prefect. He sent soldiers and priests to persuade the saint to make sacrifices to the emperor's gods. But far from persuading her, these soldiers and these priests alike were persuaded by Cecilia to be baptized to the glory of God.

Angry and yet angrier, the prefect brought Cecilia before the Roman court and commanded her to revoke her faith. But (and who could believe this?) the young woman's laughter sounded like bells, and her quick wit caused the prefect to trip over his words.

His face swelled purple, and he yelled at his soldiers, "Humiliate the woman! And then suffocate her in her bathroom!"

When that too had failed, the prefect ordered men to feed a furnace with such a great load of wood that it burned seven times hotter than it had ever burned before.

Yet Saint Cecilia withstood the flames for a day and a night.

In the end, she was martyred. She was beheaded, and yet it was said that her body gave forth the scent of spices.

Gabriel and Mary

Gabriel, an angel of the Lord, appeared to a young virgin, Mary, and announced that she would bear a baby—she and the Holy Spirit together. After the angel had vanished, Mary was transformed. She threw out her arms, and kicked up her heels, and twirled and danced, then hurried south from Nazareth to the house of her cousin Elizabeth.

"O magnify the Lord!"

Paul's Transformation

Over and over, Paul told the story of his own transformation: "While I was on my way to Damascus, it was about noon when a great light from heaven suddenly shone about me and knocked me down to the ground."

A Story of Divine Transformation

The following story recounts one of my own personal experiences. Doubtless you too will remember something of the same sort of experience.

A story of a divine transformation can happen more than once in a life. On the other hand, it might happen once only. Consider the man or the woman who, having just listened to a powerful come-to-Jesus sermon, went forward to confess and to give themselves wholly unto Jesus. There and then, they experienced a sudden, breathtaking, and transformational light not unlike what Paul experienced on his way to Damascus. They laid down the heavy burden of their sins and went out of the tent, rejoicing.

This next story presents my own experience and my own transformation.

Robert Jefferson was not a member of Grace Lutheran Church. He lived in a room of a swaybacked shotgun house on Gum Street four houses down from the church. The mild-mannered, dirt-poor fellow had trouble supporting himself. Therefore, the Mission of Grace, a Grace Lutheran Church outreach program, helped him out by giving him cast-off clothes, used shoes, coffee, loaves of bread, sticks of butter, cans of soup, a small electric hot plate, and a pan in which he fried eggs.

Wherever Robert walked, he walked within a global atmosphere of alcohol. And he walked with a cane that wasn't really a cane. It was the skinny shaft of an umbrella from which he'd stripped off both its cloth and its metal ribs. I often wondered what could be the purpose of something that couldn't hold up the weight of a nickel.

And even before you saw him coming around a corner, you could hear him by the sound of that cane's *tippy-tippy-tap-taps* on the sidewalk.

It happened one day, as I was hurrying to the church building past Robert's house with a newspaper over my head on account of a drizzling rain, that I heard a startling cry, "What's happenin', Reverent?" Right. Robert. Standing in his doorway.

He yelled, "What's happenin', Reverent?" A flock of starlings exploded from trees, and I was halted by that yell.

"C'me on in!" Robert called. "I got sumpin' to show you."

Sweet Robert Jefferson, whom Grace Church propped up in all his leaning places.

I relented and joined him in his room.

"Make it quick," I said. "I've got to get back to work."

He pointed to a nail on the wall and said, "Rest your coat, Rev?"

My coat was no coat at all. It was a wet windbreaker. I kept it on.

Robert hooked his noncane cane on the nail.

There was the scribble of a blanket on his naked mattress, and a wooden table, and a slouching, well-worn couch. The room had an ancient porcelain sink that was both attached to a wall and standing on two porcelain legs. Under the sink I saw a large cardboard box.

I said, "What do you want to show me?"

"Awright, awright," he said and kneeled down before the sink and pulled out that cardboard box, then stood and spread his arms as if he were a rich merchant showing off his wares.

"Anythin', Rev," he said expansively. "I been thinkin' on things an' done come to a idee how to pay y'all back for your Christian kindnesses."

The box held a hodgepodge of stuff: Mason jars, a cordless radio, a bicycle tire, returnable beer bottles, a BIC cigarette lighter, a magazine showing a scantily clad Bunny of the Month, a trivet that lacked one of its legs.

"Anythin' you want," Robert said. "Anythin' and she's yours."

"There's no need to pay us back," I said. "We do what we do in the name of Jesus Christ, our Savior."

Robert frowned and tugged his earlobe, perhaps contemplating what I'd just said. I took the opportunity to walk out of his alcohol-suffused room.

On Sunday, I realized that Robert's contemplation had led him to a good "idee."

While I was preaching in the aisle, Robert appeared at the back of Grace's small nave with a half-moonlike smile. He had picked out his hair into two peaks. He'd made himself presentable by having dressed in a Goodwill suit too big for his child-sized body.

Now he came (*tippy-tippy-tap-tap*) up the aisle, nodding his twin, steeple-peaked hair to the members as he passed them. "Pleased to meet choo," he said. "Right, pleased to meet choo," he said, disconcerting the people.

When he'd come close to me, he bowed and then shuffled past the knees in the second pew on my left: "'Scuse me. 'Scuse me." Robert sat down in an empty space in the middle of the pew, laid his bumbershoot cane at his feet, then looked up with a face expecting what? Perhaps a good shouting-in-the-Lord sermon.

I returned to my sober sermon: illustration, theology. Illustration, more theology.

Soon, I became aware of a soft, rhythmic sound to my left.

Robert was tapping his toes and rocking back and forth to some interior music.

A drop of sweat trickled down my backbone.

Keep preaching, Rev. Wangerin. Preach louder and faster.

Suddenly, Robert threw up his hands and cried, "Ah'm a-gonna pray!"

The shock of that cry froze my bones as if they were icicles.

And Robert, too, seemed stunned by his outburst.

"Yessir!" he cried, nodding his hair picked out in double peaks. "Yessir, ah'm a-gonna pray!"

There was nothing for it but to rush to the pew in front of this frightful interruption. I grabbed the back of the pew and leaned close to Robert's face and said, "Robert, you can't pray!"

He blinked at me. "Can't pray?" he asked.

"No," I said. "We have a time to pray."

Carefully, like a mother who has just gotten her baby to sleep, I stepped back into the aisle and rode my sermon to its "Amen."

But Robert wasn't finished. Turning from one parishioner after another, he said, "Sorry. Sorry. I didn't know y'all had a *time* to pray."

I crept back into the chancel and sat and opened the hymnbook, and the organist began to play: "Jesus, sinners doth receive."

After the hymn, I stood up, and faced the altar, and took the two collection plates in either hand, and I then turned, expecting to see the ushers to receive the plates. They *were* there but perplexed, for in front of them stood Robert in his overlarge suit.

When he saw the collection plates, he performed an act that, if it weren't true, would have been a lachrymose sentimentality.

He pulled a well-worn dollar bill from his pocket and laid it on a collection plate and turned and walked with dignity toward the back of the church, saying, "Naw. I ain't a-gonna pray for you no more."

Tippy-tippy-tap-tap, he left the church and me.

Thus my transformation. God had been in this thing.

God had confronted me, had opened my eyes to my liturgical hardheadedness, and I finally understood what Robert's cane held up—the airy feathers of that dove, the Holy Spirit, and I repented.

Now, when I came to preach the Robert story on Pentecost, I reduced it to a tight outline by which I illuminated the Gospel of John 14:8–17 with a special attention to verse 17: "This is the Spirit of truth, whom the world cannot receive, because it neither sees him nor knows him."

I paused and scanned the congregation, then spoke my own words:

"I was a citizen of the worldly order. I had not received the Spirit of Truth because I too hadn't yet seen him or known him—not until the whiskey-wise Robert Jefferson had revealed to me that the Spirit of Jesus Christ abides with us and within us and by whose grace we become citizens of the Kingdom of the Divine."

Marie, yow quen, yow moder, yow mayden briht,
Yow wilt, yow canst, yow art of miht:
Yow lyf, yow love, yow hope of blisse,
In sinne, in sorwe, in need, us wisse.[1]

12

Personal Histories

Personal histories can be stories passed down from generation to generation. The Holocaust: "Let it never be forgotten." Slavery: "Children, you must know the source of the racism that exists today." Immigration: "Remember the legacies of our forebears: Germans who crossed the Atlantic in the nineteenth century, Irish during the potato famine, Latin Americans fleeing dictatorships, Middle Eastern peoples trying to escape wars and bombings and the wiping out of their villages, immigrants who are stopped at the border, where guards refuse to grant them an entrance into the golden America."

But they may be histories too of such happy times as childbirth and birthdays, when we tell our children what sorts of kids they used to be; marriages (showing our wedding pictures to our friends and neighbors); stories about the lives and the deeds of our grandparents. Rags to riches. Victorious athletic competitions.

Such stories as these can create a fresh intimacy between storytelling preachers and their rapt congregations. And because they arise from preachers' lifeblood, they can also animate their congregations.

Saint Augustine scattered his own experiences throughout his sermons. An example is the sermon he preached in his thirteenth Christmas message:

I was out of town at the time. When I returned, I heard the sorry news from our Presbyters. They were upset by the sinful way those Christians conducted themselves. Acting in accordance with Church law, they handed out some pretty stiff disciplines to the ringleaders. Of course, as with all perpetrators, you didn't feel like you'd done a thing wrong. Yes, I've heard your mumbling and grumbling till I'm sick of it.[1]

In a mere six lines, an African American man sings a song about his weariness, a poem about his labors that ends with the divine value of his life:

Dis sun are hot,
Dis hoe are heavy,
Dis grass grow furder den I can reach;
An' as I looks
At dis Cotton fiel',
I thinks I mus' 'a' been called to preach.[2]

Likewise, Selma G. Lanes writes in her book *The Art of Maurice Sendak*, "Maurice Sendak had several fragmentary situations in mind for his first picture book." She refers to Sendak's comment that "all successful fantasy . . . must be rooted in living fact."[3]

An idea for his picture book *Where the Wild Things Are* sprang from a personal experience taken from his childhood. When he was a boy, he did not like his Brooklyn relatives who would visit his mother and dine on one of her Saturday meals. These people caused Sendak's nerves to go taut with distress. Furthermore, he had to wear formal and uncomfortable clothes.

Sendak remembered how an aunt leaned across the table and pinched his cheek, saying something like, "You're so cute I could just eat you up." *Eaten?* A frightening prospect.

Perhaps Sendak imagined that his relatives were monsters whom he then, and later in his life, mastered by telling a story about a boy who made *friends* with the monsters. *Where the Wild Things Are* changed the nightmarish fears of children into dreams of victory.

Though the following is a poem, it works as well as a story. E. E. Cummings recalls his father and fashions a poem according to the memory of his life with his father. Though the poet's language and his imagery are startling, his tone is gentle and affectionate:

> *my father moved through dooms of love*
> *through sames of am through haves of give,*
> *singing each morning out of each night*
> *my father moved through depths of height. . . .*
>
> *joy was his song and joy so pure*
> *a heart of star by him could steer*
> *and pure so now and now so yes*
> *the wrists of twilight would rejoice.*

And the final verse:

> *and nothing quite so least as truth—*
> *I say though hate were why men breathe—*
> *because my father lived his soul*
> *love is the whole and more than all.*[4]

The phrase "through haves of give" reminds me of Jesus's words: "It is better to give than to receive."

We can't, of course, tell our stories with Cummings's startling language or with his well-turned visual images. But we can relate our common experiences to our congregations with the same love and affection for them even as we have loved the men and women in our past lives.

Furthermore, we should be careful not to tell such stories in dull, fuzzy, abstract, or myopic ways. Our listeners need to see and hear and feel the tale in order to experience it. Details!

In the week before her ninetieth birthday, Miz Mary Moore took sick and died of the Covid-19 virus. Years ago, she had told her children and her grandchildren and her great-grandchild—and me—the story of the death of her own grandmother.

The woman had worked as a cleaning maid in an ancient, spacious hotel in downtown Evansville, Indiana. It might be said that she was only a little younger than the hotel itself.

The woman's long life walking Evansville's mean streets had made her wary of thugs and thieves. Therefore, she kept her paper money in a pouch strung around her neck and concealed under her clean but well-worn shirts.

One evening after her shift was over, the elderly woman was walking home when a young switched-skinny jumped out in front of her, brandishing a serrated kitchen knife and whining, "I gonna cut you, you don't gimme yo' cash money!"

Mary's grandma was nothing if not self-reliant and headstrong. "Get outa my face!" she snapped.

The fellow was vibrating, hopped up on some sort of drug.

She said, "Run off, little boy, or I'm a-gonna tell yo' mama."

The teenager grabbed her shirt and tore it from her shoulders down to her waist. Then he went after her pouch string with his knife. Its swipe pierced the upper-left quadrant of her chest.

When that jittery fellow yanked it out, they both heard a sharp *snap!* Blood flowed. And the point had cracked off its blade, lodged in one of the old woman's bones.

That night when Mary wandered into the kitchen, she saw her grandmother leaning over the sink, naked from her waist up, and washing some crusted blood from her chest.

"Mamma! What happened?"

"Nothin' to worry yo' little head about, Sugar."

Suddenly, the scab broke open and a spurt of blood shot into the sink, scaring Mary.

"Grandma! You've got to go to the hospital!"

The woman turned the faucet on to drain the blood away: "Ain't no 'got to.' All's I needs—go an' get me a butterfly bandage."

After June had become November, the old woman was coughing—a deep-chested, wet, and rumbling cough. And she kept darkening her handkerchief with globs of red blood.

She touched the old scar and ran her finger from the scar to the left side of her breastbone.

Mary was there. Her grandmother said to her, "It's on the move, Sugar."

The harder she coughed, the greater the run of blood, until she had grown pale and bone weary.

There was no help for it now. The old woman was taken by ambulance to Welborn Hospital. They X-rayed her chest. The shadows proved that she'd been right. With every breath she took, the knifepoint had been cutting through her lung and had begun to stipple her heart.

The physician said to her, "I'm sorry. I have to tell you that it is a small piece of metal too little to be surgically removed."

Home again, Mary sat beside her grandma's bed, wiping her forehead with a cool, moist cloth.

Softly, almost inaudibly, Mary heard the dying woman sing a spiritual:

And when I come to die,
And when I come to die,

Oh, when I come to die,
Give me Jesus.

Mary and I were sitting in my tiny church office when she told me her story, and her grandmother became my grandmother too.

There are a number of biblical texts that can be illuminated by a shortened version of this story. Among them might be the first lesson for the second Sunday after Pentecost, Isaiah 55:10–13, especially the twelfth verse:

For you shall go out in joy,
    and be led back in peace;
the mountains and the hills before you
    shall burst into song,
        and all the trees of the field shall clap their hands.

And then there is this personal experience that Helen Milholland shaped into a poem while living in Winterset, Iowa, 1890. Her experience is ours to read, and by reading it, we can enter her context and walk beside her:

A new voice in church. I turned around to look.
A colored boy, high-cheeked and handsome,
his head thrown back, his eyes closed,
a well-groomed moustache. Well, it was love,
so to speak, at first sight. I asked John
to speak to him after the service. He was tall,
slender, shabbily dressed but clean
and well-smelling. He wore a snapdragon,
I remember that it was yellow and purple,
in his lapel. When our eyes met,
I knew it was mutual. But he looked

at John, and at everyone else
who welcomed him in the doorway,
with the same forever.
We asked him home,
talked with him. Then John,
my dearest John, I'd never known
such pride in him: yes you will
go to college; yes you will
get an education; God
has something big
in store for you; I'll talk
to the president of Simpson College
myself if I have to.
When my eyes met John's
just after he spoke those words,
that was when I knew,
I meant what I said when I married him.

I was about ten years old. Dad was the pastor of Immanuel Lutheran Church in Grand Forks, North Dakota. He sat me down and told me a story about his grandfather Rev. Albert Wangerin and about his own transformation, which took place when he too was ten.

All his life, all through the fifty years of his ministry, Rev. Albert served Zion Lutheran Church in a town near Sollitt, Illinois.

Dad spent summers with his grandfather. The old man invited the young boy to ride in his buggy with him when he stopped to see members of his congregation—the sick and the infirm and the bedbound, farmers whose crops had withered in a drought, mothers after a difficult pregnancy, and others for other reasons.

Albert's horse's name was Sleepy. And the name of the energetic dog that chased after the buggy was Tucky, short for Kentucky.

One Sunday afternoon, the pastor and his grandson visited an old, wrinkled, unconscious, and dying woman. Young Walt watched how his grandpa served the old woman.

He prayed. He read Scripture passages to her: "O death, where *is* thy sting?" (1 Cor 15:55 KJV). And he granted her an easeful death by singing softly a German hymn:

Müde bin ich, geh zur ruh,
Schlieisse meine Aeuglein zu:
Vater, lass die Auglein dein
Uber meinem Bette sein.

Tired am I and need to rest.
Close thou me my little eyes:
Father, let your eyes divine
Watch over this bed of mine.

Rev. Albert opened the small black communion box that he carried when visiting housebound or bedbound members of the congregation. He plucked out a wafer and poured a little wine into a little chalice. He broke off a bit of the wafer, and dipped it into the wine, and touched it to his forefinger, then touched it to the old woman's tongue. This Eucharist was her last rites.

After this story, Dad explained the transformation caused by his grandfather's pastoral service.

"It was then that I determined to follow my grandfather Albert into the ministry."

In her biography, Bessie Jones writes this story, a remembrance to be read by her descendants. My version of her story will change a thing or two:

I was born in Smithville, Georgia, on February 8, 1902. My mother never had any other children, and I grew up as an only child.

Elizabeth, which was my great-grandmama's name—she stayed in Smithville. My mother had a long name—Abby Lou Frances. At home up around Buena Vista, they called her Abby. But down here on the coast, they called her Miss Frances. Now, Abby, that's God's name. Like my own name.

My grandmama never was married. She never did marry, but she had her share of children. My momma say I took after her, 'cause I didn't never want to marry. I didn't prefer marrying. My momma say that's the way *her* mother was. Say she hadn't look for no marriage at all. She had her freedom. And then when she had it, she finished righteous. Told them the time of her going and where she was going to.

She was leaving that evening at three o'clock, and just before she died, she was singing a song about get on board li'l chillum.

What I'm saying is that all those things like that didn't send my grandmother to hell just because she didn't marry a man. She raised her chillum; she did them well.

Pa and them used to say that spirits of the dead most always visit back to the places where they passed away, and I do believe that they do come back sometimes.

When I first moved into the house I'm in now, I used to sleep in the front room on account it was easy to get to the telephone.

One night I was asleep there, and in my sleep, it appeared that somebody was sitting on my pillow. I don't like for anybody to sit on my pillow, period. So I pushed myself back. I pushed myself back so hard I woke myself.

And he spoke so plain I could hear it all in the house: "You don't know who it is sitting here." It kind of scared me. It shook me so until I was scared to go to bed the next night. That voice spoke all over the whole room. But I prayed it off. I never tried to find out who he was either.

13

Factual Historical Stories

These stories not only probe our pasts. When we tell them and when the members of our congregations hear them and experience them and identify with one of their characters, they may recognize their own deepest selves.

Pliny the Younger wrote a history about the eruption of Mount Vesuvius. Likewise, we might apply that eruption to, say, the eruptions of a politician.

Abraham Lincoln's Emancipation Proclamation allows us to be the president, or a slave, or a slave set free.

Who are we? Who can we be? Crusaders? Pilots, soldiers, or gunners in the Second World War? The enemy, Germans who led Jews to the gas chambers? Or one of the Jews?

Our past forms us.

Each case gives us the opportunity to delve into our own personhoods—moral and immoral, sometimes proud and sometimes humble, brave and timid, scholars and idiots, gentle people and downright nasty people, faithful and faithless by turns.

You have a responsibility to tell history because people forget history.

—Leslie Brody, quoted in Brenda Miller
and Suzanne Paola, *Tell It Slant*

In 1 Samuel 16:23, David takes up his lyre and plays it with a skill, plays such a tranquil music that it eases King Saul's despondency, his half-mad anxieties, casting out the evil spirits that hector him.

This relationship begins good and healthily—until Saul's behavior and his jealousies make him erratic and dangerous. When the people praise David's victories, Saul hurls a spear at David, but it splinters against the wall, and his failure vexes him all the more.

I have been jealous. When my plans—to publish a book, to promote it, to earn the praise of people—have been shattered against the obstinate rock of an editor's indifferent rejection, I've felt in my soul something like King Saul's hostility. No spear in my hand. But a private and unspoken enmity.

On the other hand, I have also been another David—a consoling pastor.

But what are we to make of the quasi-political and martial nature of our forebears' hymns such as "Onward Christian Soldiers, Marching as to War" and "Bring Peace to Earth Again"? Although this last hymn ends with the words "Bring peace to the earth again," it begins with stark images of war:

> Where armies scourge the countryside, and people flee in fear,
> where sirens through flaming night, and death is ever near.
>
> Where anger festers in the heart, and strikes with cruel hand;
> Where violence stalks the troubled streets, and terror haunts the land.[1]

Do we really want to identify with such military attitudes?

And what about "The Battle Hymn of the Republic" and our proud, victorious paean "O say, can you see by the dawn's early light . . ."?

Why not conform ourselves to the historical John Milton and his "Sonnet 19"?

> *When I consider how my light is spent*
>   *Ere half my days in this dark world and wide,*
>   *And that one talent which is death to hide*
>   *Lodged with me useless, though my soul more bent*
>
> *To serve therewith my Maker, and present*
>   *My true account, lest he returning chide,*
>   *"Doth God exact day-labor, light denied?"*
>   *I fondly ask. But patience, to prevent*
>
> *That murmur, soon replies, "God doth not need*
>   *Either man's yoke or his own gifts. Who best*
>   *Bear his mild yoke, they serve him best. His state*
>
> *Is Kingly: thousands at his bidding speed,*
>   *And post o're land and ocean without rest;*
>   *They also serve who only stand and wait."*

On the other hand, the history of the arrogant, self-assertive general Douglas MacArthur is for us a cautionary tale from its true beginning when he graduated with the highest honors from West Point in 1903 to its ending in 1951, when Harry S. Truman demanded the general's resignation.

    Take a lesson, colleagues: MacArthur's rise and fall should not denote our own.

Rather, we might base our lives, our ministries, our preaching, and our stories on the history of the French king Louis IX.

He was a sincere and unbigoted Christian. Before his coronation, he'd been a splendid and generous knight. And after he had ascended the throne, Louis became a king who strove never to wrong any of his subjects, neither the poorest peasant nor the richest noble.

A pious king and a protector of the church, just as we ought to serve and protect our congregations from error and from the assaults of the devil.

In spite of his fits of temper and his sometime aggressions, Louis ruled his kingdom as a just and impartial judge. He loved his wife, Margaret, eagerly and ardently, an unusual coupling in the days when marriages were made for political reasons. Witness: this king and his queen produced eleven children together.

During a serious case of malaria, Louis decided to take up the cross of Christ and to lead his barons and his army to the Holy Land—the Seventh Crusade.

The situation was dire. Muslims ruled Jerusalem, and the Sultan of Egypt had seized Damascus. Louis sailed east with a hundred ships and thirty thousand knights and bowmen and foot soldiers.

Upon his arrival, the king was one of the first to leap ashore.

Can we, too, in spite of our iniquities, place our faith in the Lamb who suffered for our salvation? Will we, too, bravely assume the cross of Christ and confront a scornful and even a belligerent world? Confront and preach against the transgressions of some of the members of our churches whose souls are infected by transgressions as hurtful as malaria? What a painful thing to do.

Or can we be genuinely pious and as genuinely equitable in our judgments?

Are we able to love as Jesus loved? Dearly, forgivingly, warmly, ardently?

14

The Jewish Haggadah

In Hebrew, the word *haggadah* means "to show. To announce. To tell. To tell a narrative story as it was told and taught in the ancient synagogues."

As a haggadah is repeated down the ages, it evolves into a legend embroidered with the tellers' inventions. A haggadah is freewheeling. It doesn't pretend to be authoritative. It is a midrash that appealed to the common folk and has often sprung from the folk themselves.

Twenty centuries ago, the historian Josephus wrote in his *Jewish Antiquities*, "Though we have been deprived of our wealth, of our cities, or of the other advantages we have, yet our Torah continues immortal."[1]

I am inspired by Dr. Fred Niedner's essay concerning a midrash structured on the biblical/historical Rachel, the beloved wife of Jacob.[2]

While Leah was bearing for her husband, Jacob, ten sons and a daughter, her sister, Rachel, remained barren, praying that the Lord would open her womb too. But God did not.

Rachel, jealous of her sister, demanded, "Jacob, give me children or I will die."

Jacob answered, "Who do you think I am? God?"

Then the Lord, the Creator, gave ear to Rachel's pleas, opening her womb after all, and she gave birth to a son whom she and her husband named Joseph.

After baby Joseph had been weened, Rachel secluded herself in her tent and once again begged for a second child.

But this time, her labor was so difficult and painful that the baby's head tore the deepest flesh of her womanhood, and blood streamed down her buttocks, and her face became as pale as the moon.

With her last breath, Rachel named her baby boy Benoni, "the son of my sorrow," then slipped away into the darkness of death.

Jacob buried his best beloved with his own tender sorrow, then memorialized her by raising a tall stone pillar over her grave, which, said the biblical narrator, still stands and may still be honored by those who pass by.

But he did not want his generations to bear a name of misery, so he renamed his small son Benjamin, "the son of my right hand, the son of good fortune."

At this point, the rabbi who was telling Rachel's story started to develop it with his own midrash.

After God had watched the destruction of Solomon's temple and had watched as Judah was driven into exile, the Lord wept burning tears.

Great Yahweh then commanded the prophet Jeremiah to call up from their graves the three ancestors of the Hebrews and a leader of the Jews: Abraham and Isaac and Jacob and Moses. Once they were standing in the presence of the Divine, they were one by one asked to "weep with me over the desolation of my people."

And each man answered properly and righteously: "O Lord my God, restore your people."

Again, God said, "Weep with me, and my people will be restored and returned to their homeland."

Abraham now shed tears, proudly saying, "It's me. I will restore the fortunes of Israel because I was most faithful and obedient when you commanded me to bind my son and lay him on a stone altar and slay him with my knife. I did what you commanded, and I had put my trust in you. Therefore, send me."

But Abraham's Lord and God said, "There is no place for arrogance in my kingdom." Father Abraham groused and stomped away.

Then Isaac was snuffling and weeping big tears. He said, "It was me! *I* believed what your angels prophesied that I and my wife were going to bear a son. And this is the proof of my faith: Rebekah did not believe what I believed. She laughed! But I was right. A baby *was* born to us. Who, Lord, is more devout and righteous and as pure and as sinless than I? Therefore, pick me."

But God said, "A liar is not righteous. When the men of Gerar saw Rebekah's beauty, they wanted to take her into their houses. But you? You were afraid that they would tear your wife away from you and hurt you and even kill you. So you lied, Isaac, and said that she was your sister."

Next, Jacob came boo-hooing and boasting about the decades he had toiled for his uncle Laban: "And what about those twenty years when I toiled and risked my life—and all for *you*, my Lord."

"Right," said the Lord. "But you feared for your *own* life because you feared that your brother, Esau, would kill you. So you sent your servants and your herds and all your possessions and even your family across the Jordan to smooth your brother's wrath before you yourself crossed the Jordan. The tears of a self-serving man mean nothing to me."

And then it was Moses who came crying crocodile tears. "God will surely honor *me*," he said, "because it was me and no one else who led the Jews out of Egypt, and I can do it again."

But God said, "Moses! Do you presume to do what is *mine* to do?"

So the four men went away dry eyed and grumpy.

Now the Lord commanded Jeremiah to call Rachel up from her grave.

Jeremiah knew of Rachel's lamentation and the bitter tears and that she had wept for her children because they were not.

Then here was Rachel, standing humbly before Yahweh, and when Yahweh told her the reason for his tears, she also shed tears of sorrow like the sorrows of the Lord, for both had lost what was dear to them.

God said, "Rachel, keep your voice from sobbing and your eyes from tears. There is a reward for one whose life was difficult and whose death was a misery."

This, the rabbi's midrash, needed no interpretation. The story was its own instruction.

Another rabbi built another midrash on the first commandment as it is written in the fifth chapter of Deuteronomy: "I am the Lord your God who brought you out of the land of Egypt, out of the house of slavery. You shall have no other gods besides Me" (vv. 6-7 NASB).

And a different rabbi began his midrash with the third day of creation.

On that day, the Creator brought forth on the earth all green and growing things and among them the cedars of Lebanon. Because the cedars' trunks were tall and strong and majestic, and because their branches formed a lattice (a fretwork of shadows on the paths below), and because their fingerlike green leaves reached halfway to heaven, they said to one another, "Come. Let us make of ourselves the four pillars planted on the four corners of the world with which to hold up the firmament."

The Creator then came down to see this thing that the cedars were doing.

"Ah," said the Lord, "vanities of vanities. These trees want to pierce and to enter into my kingdom. They think that there is nothing that they cannot do."

This rabbi concluded his midrash by quoting the words of the prophet Isaiah: "The Lord of hosts has a day against all that is proud and lofty, against all that is lifted up and high; against all the cedars of Lebanon" (2:12-13).

These are midrashim of old. But there are also midrashim told in and about this present time. Many of these stories and the experiences engendered in their listeners are meant to lead them into moral and righteous paths.

But some are told by people ignorant of their story's deleterious effect.

An example is the following:

In the 1980s, men who lived in Greenwich Village began to die from a mysterious disease. The symptoms could be ghastly. The men grew tired and then so very tired that they could not rise from their beds. Their lymph glands swelled. After restless nights, they'd wake on sheets sopping with their sweat. And their feet and their faces developed running lesions. Such a sad irony because their bodies were killing their own bodies.

Soon their disease was diagnosed as HIV/AIDS.

By March 1983, 1,112 persons had contracted AIDS, and their friends and their lovers mourned for the four hundred who had already died.

Like the lepers in the days of Jesus who were made to cry, "Unclean! Unclean!" so it was with the gays in the 1980s. They too were shunned by people who feared them, people who blamed them for spreading their frightful disease.

The last straw broke when a ten-year-old boy living in northern Indiana was diagnosed as also having contracted HIV/AIDS.

Rev. Irvin Baxter Jr. (not his name) was a widely watched televangelist. He built a broadcasting system that drew thousands and thousands of people to their television sets by his apocalyptic prophesies. The man told stories—short midrashim—about the divine punishments that God was meting out to a nation because it tolerated homosexuality and gay marriages and the unmarried couples who lived in sin: "A sinful nation! People laden with iniquities! Offspring who do evil! Children who deal corruptly! Your country will lie desolate! God is ready to burn your cities with fire!"

On the other hand, there was in Evansville, Indiana, a pastor whose ministry was kind and his church a vast congregation. This man never fulminated. He spoke in the manner of an affectionate school teacher.

He too preached a story critical of homosexuality: "These days are like the days when lepers cried, 'Unclean! Unclean!'"

Yet when I went to him and explained his error, saying, "Jesus cherished everyone, foreigners, those who were not Jews, the Gadarene demoniac, the Canaanite woman who said, 'Have mercy on me, Lord, Son of David. My daughter is tormented by a demon,'" this good pastor was persuaded to change his attitude.

When we pastors choose to work a midrash into our sermons, it's important first to decide whether it is or it isn't a midrash. If it is, we'll know how to develop it with our own applicable inventions. But if it isn't, it will baffle our congregations as though the story were a piecemeal crumble of trivialities.

15

Stories That Compose an Entire Sermon

Acts 2 reports that on the day of Pentecost, Peter preached a sermon, the full first part of which consisted of a historical story:

> Men of Judea and all who live in Jerusalem, . . . "In the last days it will be, God declares, that I will pour out my Spirit upon all flesh. . . ." You that are Israelites, listen to what I have to say: Jesus of Nazareth, a man attested to you by God with deeds of power, wonders, and signs that God did through him among you . . . God raised him up, having freed him from death. (Acts 2:14, 17, 22, 24)

In the three Synoptic Gospels, Jesus's parables mostly stand alone. He interprets only two of them: the seeds and the sower and the wheat and the tares. And sometimes he will indicate the parables' substance and context first. A lawyer asks, "Who is my neighbor?" (Luke 10:29). And the Lord answers with the parable of the Good Samaritan without a commentary or an explanation.

The story-sermons preached by Peter and Jesus were then and there.

But we can preach in the here and now, also without embellishments.

Regarding such sermons, David Buttrick writes that the story ought to be told "in the mode of immediacy."[1] And some of us who are blessed with keen congregations can trust that they will understand a scriptural story just as it is, to enter it and to experience it by becoming one of its characters.

Shortly before the St. Louis Seminary sent Grace Lutheran Church a woman intern, I prepared the congregation to accept a female by asking a Methodist pastor, a woman named Nadia, to preach a series of Wednesday-night Lenten sermons. Each of her sermons told a tale taken from the Old Testament—the covenants that God established first with the Hebrews and then with the Jews, with Noah, Abraham, Jacob, King David. Nadia's last story looked forward to the New Testament, to the Easter covenant to be celebrated at the end of Lent.

My plan and my preparation succeeded. The congregants of Grace Church had been ready to complain. But after the cheerful Cheri Johnson arrived and preached and ministered to them, they were happy to receive her.

There was little difference between Nadia's Lenten tales and my father's. He, too, preached a series of Lenten sermons. Each of his stories began and ended the sermon with nothing, neither an interpretation nor an explanation, in between. They recounted the experiences of the people who witnessed Christ's passion.

But he didn't tell his stories in the third person—"they," "he," "she." Rather, he told them in the first person. He *was* the thick-skulled Simon Peter, and the Beloved Disciple, and even Judas, and on Good Friday, he was the weeping Mary Magdalene.

When I became a pastor in my own right, I preached the parable of the prodigal son and the waiting father. That story composed the whole of my sermon, and I told it as happening in the here and the now. In this case, I didn't preach it to my congregation. I preached it to one young fellow who was much in need of it.

Junie Piper was lying face down and filthy in a jail cell. His afro had been crushed on one side, and he was wearing nothing but his underwear. His real name was Melvin Piper Jr., after his father, Melvin Piper Sr. In order to distinguish between the two, his parents nicked his name and called him Junie.

I'd first met Junie in his mother's living room. A lean and tallish and melancholy young man. His eyes were attractive, as liquid brown as the eyes of a fawn. His hair had been neatly picked out. But when I shook his hand, I felt limpid fingers and a palm both soft and damp.

While Junie stood looking vaguely out of the living room's bay window, his mother chatted about this thing and that. "Mah boy," she said, "he was a mama-obedient boy. Growed up to be a cook, done cooked for the navy. What Ah'm sayin', he a *good* cook."

Lola cast an eye at her son. "Was a misery," she said. "Was a affliction and a misery."

Junie turned from the window and left the room.

His mother bemoaned her misery, saying, "Done was kicked out o' the navy, was mah Junie, and them complainin' about 'lazy,' an' what they say, 'slack' an' 'don't never obey commands.'

"But what *I* say, he only just a thoughty man. Always was."

Lola stood up. "Coffee, Reverent?"

"That would be nice."

I spent the time trying to figure out how best to tell her the reason I'd come. But when the woman returned, it was she who introduced the topic.

The coffee that she set on the tea table before me came in a well-designed porcelain cup.

She said, "Might-be you is wonderin' why I ain't been showin' mah face in church of a Sunday mornin'."

"Yes," I said. "I've been aware of your absence."

"Well," she said, "it account of mah false teeth. Hoo. What it is, I be lookin' here and there but cain't never find them nowhere."

I think it was two weeks later when Lola telephoned me in a hard-breathing panic.

Junie had rolled a man "ret there," she said. "Ret there in front o' the county jail! Nose candy's what they sayin'. But I don't set no store by what the poh-lice is sayin'. Sayin' they done found a shootin' gun in his pocket. They's liars, Reverent! Junie, he got a old cap gun from when he was itty bitty."

I wasted no time. Without changing my clothes, I drove to the county jail.

That building consisted of three stories. On the first floor, a sergeant sat behind a desk, answering questions, informing people that he was not, and this place was not, the place to pay for traffic tickets. Nor was the sergeant much interested when handcuffed men or women were being led away to be fingerprinted and to have their pictures taken. "Face front. Now face to the side."

Behind this sergeant were several detectives who sat at gray metal desks, talking on their telephones, taking notes, typing official reports, drinking Cokes or coffee, chatting, tossing jokes at one another, and laughing.

On the building's second and third floors were cells for criminals, perps, men waiting to be tried.

Aloof and lazy, the desk sergeant asked what I wanted.

"I've come to visit Junie Piper."

He gave me the once-over and then said that visiting hours were Tuesdays and Thursdays, one to three o'clock. "This," he said, "is Wednesday."

I said that I was Junie Piper's pastor.

"Right," he said. "And I'm Jesus."

Oh, I got it. He thought that pastors don't wear jeans and a sweatshirt.

I took out my billfold and showed him the card that identified me as a minister in the Evangelical Lutheran Church in America.

He examined my card and said, "Wait a minute," then punched a digit on his telephone. He waited, tapping the point of his pencil on the surface of his desk, and then spoke into the receiver: "Hey, Jerry. There's a Pastor Wangerin down here. Wants to talk to a Junie Piper. You got that name on your list?"

After a short minute, the sergeant pressed the phone to his breast and said, "Sorry, Father. Jerry can't find that name on his list."

It occurred to me, then, that Junie's real name was *Melvin* Piper, so I said, "Try Melvin Piper Jr."

And that was the ticket. The sergeant said, "Stand over by that elevator and wait."

But there weren't buttons with arrows pointing up or down. The elevator took its own sweet time. Finally, its door slid open. The elevator's interior was claustrophobic—three padded walls and a dim light bulb caged in the ceiling.

When the door slid open again, I stepped out into a plain, gray, cinder-blocked room. The wall to my left showed several rows of lockers with their doors closed. Directly across from me sat a guard behind what must have been a bulletproof window, and in the window was a metal, louvered speaking hole.

Jerry glanced down at a clipboard and then up at me and said, "You're here for Melvin Piper, right, Father?"

"Yes," I said. "But not a 'father.' I'm a Lutheran pastor."

I had expected this guard to be like other guards that I had met—impersonal, disinterested, abrupt. But Jerry had kindly eyes and an amiable disposition.

"Put your coins and your wallet in one of those lockers, anything sharp. And matches, if you have them." Matches?

"Lock it," he said, "and keep the key."

Jerry stood up. "Wait here," he said and vanished.

A whole lot of waiting going on.

After a short minute, I heard a scratching at a metal door that I hadn't noticed before.

The door opened. Jerry stepped out with a ring of keys that hung from his belt and jingled.

He said, "Reverend, I hope you can bring the fellow out of his blue funk. He doesn't talk. He doesn't eat. He doesn't even move." Jerry turned to the doorway and said, "Follow me."

We walked down a long hallway lit by bloodless fluorescent light bulbs that were recessed in the ceiling. To our left side was a series of windows giving out to the city and its buildings. To our right was a long row of jail cells, each the duplicate of the others: dark lairs eight feet deep and six feet wide, lidless aluminum toilets in the back, an aluminum sink, an aluminum shelf with a small radio, and a cabinet for the prisoners' personal items. Against the right-hand wall were narrow beds, and jail-issue blankets, and thin mattresses. Between the beds and the left wall were floor spaces equal to the width of the beds.

Finally, Jerry stopped in front of one of these cells and said, "Melvin, here's your preacher. You best listen to him." Then he said to me, "Fifteen minutes and I'll be back."

Junie broke my heart. He was, as I've already said, lying face down on the floor between the bed and the wall, his head close to the steel bars, his face buried in the crook of an arm. I smelled the stink of human sweat.

"Junie?" I asked. "Do you remember me?"

No movement. No answer.

I knelt down and said, "We met in your mother's living room, remember?"

For all I knew, the young man was comatose.

"I'm your mother's pastor," I said. "I hope that I can be your pastor too."

I have a prayer I pray when my day has been strenuous and fruitless. Or when I can't sleep because the faces of the people I've wronged are passing before my eyes.

Then I'll pray my prayer in Latin. It gives me the sense of a complete and personal privacy. Moreover, the Latinate vowels are a consolation.

"Illumina, quaesumus, Domine, tenebras nostras."

But hoping that Junie, even in his state, might hear me after all, I prayed the prayer in English:

"Enlighten our darkness, O Lord, and defend us from the perils and the dangers of this insidious night."

It seemed no more than a minute when I heard Jerry's keys jingling in the hallway.

The next day, I arrived at the county building wearing my black shirt and my clerical collar so no one would question my right to be there. And this time, I brought my Bible.

Junie must have moved between yesterday and today. He was still lying on the floor, but there was a tray that had been set on the floor beside him. A sandwich and potato chips and a pickle and Coke in a paper cup. He hadn't touched the food, but I saw that he had drunk half of the Coke.

As I had yesterday, so now I knelt close to the cell's bars. This time, however, I risked a gesture that, I don't know, might frighten Junie. I reached into the cell and touched his shoulder. Surely he felt that, but he didn't move.

What else? I opened my Bible to the fifteenth chapter in Luke and began to read—to preach, as it were—a sermon that was, word for word, the parable of the prodigal son.

Once more, Jerry's jangling keys signaled that my time was up.

After that day, my ministerial duties required much of my attention. I could visit Junie only once or twice a week.

He was eating now. I found him sitting on the side of his bed. But he remained silent, gazing at his hands folded between his knees and never raising his eyes to look at me.

By now Jerry had generously allowed me to visit Junie for longer and longer periods of time. One day, I spent time chit-chatting about extraneous things: "What do you like to cook?" And "Can I have your recipes?" Like I said, this and that.

I said, "Your mother tells me that she doesn't come to church because she can't find her teeth. But I bet she crunches candy."

Junie chuckled!

I grinned and asked, "What's so funny?"

Finally, the young man looked at me with his fawn-liquid eyes and shook his head.

"What?" I asked.

Junie murmured, "Don't never lose them."

Oh, what a happy afternoon! And what an opportunity!

Once more, I preached the parable of the prodigal, this time enriching it with my own imagined details.

"So," I began, "there's this young fellow named Prodigal, a light-skinned and tallish man and so shiftless that he never lifts a finger to help his daddy around the house. What he *does* do, he goes to clubs and listens to rap music. He buys silk shirts and heavy silver chains that he hangs around his neck. He sits on barstools, buying whiskeys for himself and yelling, 'Drinks all around!' He's making friends with his father's money. 'And hamburgers and french fries all around!'

"Now, Prodigal's daddy is a dark-skinned fireplug of a man, a very rich and practical businessman. He saves his money and buys only the things that he needs. He lives a plain life, Junie. *His* name is Love, and loving is what he does.

"One night, Prodigal is hunkering down in the backseat of his secondhand Chevy, kissing this willing young woman, unlatching her bra, you know, and running his hands down her panties. He's breathing hard. But that young woman is breathing normally.

"Just before she lets him have his way with her, she puts her mouth close to his ear and whispers, 'Hey, baby, buy me a Jaguar.'

"Prodigal thinks to himself, 'A Jaguar?' And that thought makes him angry because his father's allowance is never enough for what Prodigal *really* wants.

"After he lets the prostitute out on the street where she sticks her head into men's car windows, Prodigal comes up with a plan.

"Come morning, he goes to his daddy and says—no, he *demands*, 'I want my inheritance. Not this month. Not next week. Tomorrow!'

"It's important, Junie, that you understand that nobody can get his inheritance until his father is dead, and the lawyer has read the man's will in front his family. You see? You get it? Prodigal is acting like his daddy is *already* dead.

"You know about sailors who get kicked out of the navy, right? It doesn't matter if they're good cooks. Some petty officer might blame them for being lazy. He might snarl, 'That guy! That fool don't obey a righteous command!'

"Well, it's the same with Prodigal, except for one important difference. He's about to kick *himself* out of his father's house. Get my meaning?

"Now, because Love loves his boy, he does what *I* would never do. He gives his son his *own* credit card.

"Prodigal wastes no time. He goes right out and buys a first-class airline ticket, and then he's flying off to Chicago.

"This young fellow rents a three-bedroom, furnished apartment on the Magnificent Mile. He cooks for himself the most costly foods. And he spends wads of money making friends. Throws parties like hallelujah! Plays rap that blares from his high-tech sound system. Oh, how the young men and women stomp the floor, dancing till their armpits are dark with sweat.

"And the feasts!

"None of that thick-crusted Chicago pizza, no. Rib eye steaks broiled blood-rare or medium or *crispy*! Corncobs roasted in their jackets; hot cross rolls, one a penny, two a penny; roasted and crusted chicken sticks; a thanksgiving banquet! Pumpkin pies, apple pies, pastries with the finest flakes. Heinekens in, I don't know, kegs! Gin and Kentucky bourbon and Jack Daniel's and, to prove that he's outrageously rich, French brandy.

"Such a jubilation in Prodigal's apartment! That dazzle of dancing. Raw jokes. Hard-playing guitars. Songs smeared with alcohol.

"By morning, Prodigal's friends are lying on his floor, sleeping in puddles of beer, snoring stinking odors, and dead drunk. The floor is littered with crunches of Fritos and kicked-off shoes and broken glass and empty bottles. Prodigal's apartment looks like alley trash.

"Now someone might say that he's living a cheerful and jolly life, until that life takes a turn for the worse.

"The landlord demands payment for the destruction of his lent-out apartment. Prodigal has to pay almost all of his money. Then the landlord kicks him out anyway. Worse goes to worst. A heat wave hits Chicago. The summer gets so hot that old people start to suffocate in their tenement rooms.

"Prodigal has maxed out his credit card. So he goes to his friends and asks them to put him up for a while. 'Just till I get back on my feet again.'

"But his friends prove that they are leeches and that they never were his friends.

"So the young man, he is wandering the mean streets in Chicago. He sleeps in the bus station until he's thrown out of that. Soon he's eating the leftovers in the bins behind restaurants.

"And then what, Junie? I think that you already know what happens then.

"One night, the cops find him sleeping in the doorway of a bank and arrest him and charge him with sticking a gun in the ribs of a man who was walking by, of mugging that man. There was no gun, of course. But the cops took the word of the white man. They printed him, and shot pictures of him, and tossed him in jail."

Now, because my story-sermon was getting long, I wondered if Junie had been paying attention, or even if he was actually listening. I couldn't tell. He had covered his face with his hands and was rocking back and forth on the side of his bed.

But I couldn't stop until I'd come to goodness and grace.

"Like I said, no gun, no evidence. So Prodigal is released, and he feels that he is nothing but ashes. It makes him mournful to remember the better days when he lived with his father.

"What if he went home? Yes, but what if his father will be like that landlord and kick him out of *his* house too? By then the poor young man has lost all hope.

"Junie, *listen* to what I have to say. Love never thought, not even for a second, that Prodigal is *not* his son.

"So this is what happened.

"One day, Love is looking out of his bedroom window, and then he bursts into tears. But these are *happy* tears.

"'Here he comes,' says Love. 'Here comes my son!'

"The man sees that Prodigal is filthy and as skinny as a stick, and his clothes are rags, and he is barefoot, and he has trouble walking.

"Prodigal's father races out of his house. He runs to his son, and throws his arms around him, and squeezes him so hard that Prodigal groans, for Love is about to break his ribs.

"Love stands back and says, 'My son, my son! I thought you were dead, but here you are!

"'Alive!'"

This was the end of my story.

I left the jail and went home filled with doubt.

It was after midnight when the telephone woke me up. I snatched the receiver from its cradle before it rang a second time and woke my wife up too.

I cleared the croak from my throat and said, "Rev. Wangerin."

An operator's crisp voice asked, "Rev. Wangerin, will you accept the charges?"

A long-distance call, then. But who would be calling at this time of night?

The voice said, "A Mr. Melvin Piper wants to speak with you."

Of course. When a telephone call comes from a jail, the charges are reversed.

"Put him on!" I cried.

There was a *click*, and I heard breathing, and that was all I heard.

"Junie?" I asked. "Is that you? Are you up? Are you talking to me?"

It was Junie, all right. He said, "Well."

"Oh, Junie, I'm so glad to hear from you!"

"Well," he said.

"Junie! Junie! Say something!"

Again he said, "Well." And then he said, "I love you."

If Junie's declaration had not been a historical fact, what I've just told you would have been a saccharine sentimentality.

Note: To say to someone "Jesus loves you" is to offer nothing more than a foggy abstraction. It can't be experienced. And to someone who doesn't really know what love *is*, that phrase is as meaningless as an illegible scrawl.

To be experienced, "Love" must be given a setting, and living characters, and the characters' actions, and an effective dialogue, and the realities of a congregation's common life.

So then let Love be God the Father, who, when he sees a baptized son or daughter in the offing, sends his only begotten Son to embrace them within the arms that once hung on a cross.

Prodigal's iniquity that had cut him off from his earthly father—and our iniquities that have cut us off from our Lord and God—is forgiven by his loving-kindness and his grace and his mercy.

Thus have Love and Love's son, Prodigal, been given a local habitation and a name.

The Virgin Mary sings of her love for humanity, that love that we crave:

> Nowe, man, have mynde on me forever.
> Loke on thy love thus languysshyng;
> Late us never fro other dissevere:
> Myne helpe ys thyne oune; crepe under my wynge.
> Thy syster is a queen, thy brother is a kynge,
> Thys heritage ys tayled; sone, come therto.
> Take me for thy wife and lerne to synge,
>   Quia amore langueo.[2]
>
> Now, man, be mindful of me forever.
> Look on your love thus languishing.
> Let us never be separated from one another.
> My help is your own. Creep under my wing.
> Your sister is a queen, your brother is a king.
> This heritage is guaranteed. Son, come thereto.
> Take me for your wife and learn to sing,
>   Because I languish for love.

There are pastors—mostly Black, some of them white—who intone their sermons. "Tonin'" is the vernacular. At some point during their sermons, these preachers might break into a rhythmic step. They may, then, start pacing left and right, preaching and preaching, until their pacing becomes a true stomp.

"Huh," they'll say between sentences. "Huh," they'll say, increasing the sound. Then "*Huh!*"—shouted loudly from the depths of their abdomens while mopping sweat from their foreheads with voluminous handkerchiefs.

"My preaching text," one particular Black pastor announced at the start of his sermon, "my text is the whole Bible!"

William B. McClain writes about an elderly African American's advice to a younger preacher:

> Start low; go slow,
>   Go high; strike fire.
>   Sit down.³

Here's a brief example of how to make a past story present and at the same time to give the congregation a sudden and immediate sense of familiarity. (Details, details, the seeing, the hearing, the touching of the thing.) She changed Matthew's language.

On the fourteenth Sunday after Pentecost, my pastor, Erica Gibson-Even, read the Gospel lesson exactly as it is found in Matthew 15:21–28:

> Just then a Canaanite woman from that region came out and started shouting, "Have mercy on me, Lord, Son of David; my daughter is tormented by a demon." But he did not answer her at all. And his disciples came and urged him, saying, "Send her away, for she keeps shouting after us." He answered, "I was sent only to the lost sheep of the house of Israel." But she came and knelt before him, saying, "Lord, help me." He answered, "It is not fair to take the children's food and throw it to the dogs." She said, "Yes, Lord, yet even the dogs eat the crumbs that fall from their masters' table." Then Jesus answered her, "Woman, great is your faith! Let it be done for you as you wish." And her daughter was healed instantly.

Then Pastor Erica invigorated Matthew's words with words of her own: "A strange woman came running across the street, screaming, 'My baby! My baby! She has a devil!'"

PART IV

Theatrics

The smiling mouth, and laughing eyen grey.

—Translated from the French of Charles d'Orléans

16

Theatrical Preachers in the Past

I believe that theatrical preaching reaches back to the rituals of various religions, what Leonel L. Mitchell says is "one in which there is commitment to the inner reality symbolized by external gesture." And again, "Love, whether of God or of the girl next door is all but impossible to express except through outward symbolic action. . . . For us, as much for primitive societies, it is a good ritual system which will enable us to find meaning in the universe and in our own lives."[1]

It isn't hard to imagine the theatrical action of John the Baptizer when he preached in the wilderness. His dramatic costume declared his person and his purpose. He was another Elijah. His food (the *action* of his eating) symbolized the life that he had chosen to live.

And his proclamations must have been histrionic: an urgency that persuaded the people of Judea to confess their sins, after which John enacted the sacred ritual of holy baptism, as well as angry accusations that he leveled at the Pharisees and the Sadducees who had also come to be baptized. How could he *not* have used visible gestures and scolding tones? "You brood of vipers!" (Matt 3:7).

When the scribes and the Pharisees brought to Jesus a woman who had been caught in adultery, his sermon began with a mute gesture: He "bent down and wrote with his finger on the ground" (John 8:6). Then he preached a brief but piercing sermon: "Let anyone among you who is without sin be the first to throw a stone at her" (John 8:7).

Likewise, the apostle Paul, who at the synagogue in Antioch "stood up and with a gesture began to speak" (Acts 13:16).

The twelfth-century philosopher, teacher, and preacher Peter Abelard was well known for his antic activities in his classrooms. James Burge writes,

> He seems to have had the ability to entertain his students. He must have mixed with performers who worked in the courts of noblemen and in the taverns, quite possibly even performing himself. . . . He seems to have had the ability to entertain his students. . . . All the accounts of his teaching (including, of course, his own) agree that his lectures were very popular. . . . Another account mentions how amusing and even funny he was.[2]

And consider George Whitefield, who arrived in America in 1740 and became the leading preacher in the Great Awakening. According to Helen Hosier,

> He dramatized both the biblical narrative and the application, spoke entirely without notes, made violent gestures, laughed, sang, and shed public tears. . . . Some said that his powers "were chiefly of the platform." . . . But "his imagination was as agile as his body, his sensitiveness to the mood of an audience unerring."[3]

17

Motion and Meaning I

The following sentence is found in Flannery O'Connor's *Mystery and Manners*: "The writer's moral sense coincides with his dramatic sense."[1]

John Gardner advises the emerging writer,

> To make us see and feel vividly what his characters see and feel—to draw us into the characters' world as if we were born to it—the writer must do more than simply make up characters and then somehow explain and authenticate them. He must shape [them] simultaneously . . . his characters, his plot and setting, each inextricably connected to the others; he must make his whole world in a single, coherent gesture, as a potter makes a pot.[2]

And Saint Augustine writes, "If, however, the hearers require to be roused rather than instructed, in order that they be diligent to do what they already know, and to bring their feelings into harmony with the truths they admit, greater vigor of speech is needed."[3]

David H. C. Read writes at length about his observations regarding the importance of the storytelling preacher's physical actions:

> In human terms the sermon must come alive. No matter how much toil and sweat has gone into the preparation, it must now be spoken with direct contact and immediacy. That means an actual rethinking in the presence of a congregation of what was laboriously worked over on paper. There must be no impression of the secondhand, of repetition of something which has already been done. This rules out straight reading, whether from a manuscript or from some point in the back of the memorizer's mind. Like an actor, the preacher has to be sensitive to his audience, knowing instinctively when they are following or when he has lost them, when they are alert and when they are tired, and he must be ready to change pace, repeat, or pause, according to the mood.[4]

Likewise, it is necessary that we preachers ought also to pay close attention to our congregation members' responses in order to adjust our stories according to their moods and their expressions.

When he was telling one of his long epics—the *Iliad* or the *Odyssey*—Homer would often repeat a "formula" word for word. This "formula" gave him the time to take the measure of his audience.

Had they been losing interest? If so, he shortened the story and charged it with a new excitement. Were they already caught up and hanging on his every word? If so, he would lengthen the tale and fill it with fresh adventures.

Let's return, now, to our own active theatrics and again to Jana Childers's *Performing the Word*:

> The thing I miss most about the Pentecostal church of my youth is not the ecstatic speech, it is the singing. In my

mind's eye, I see Buddy Ellison on a humid Sunday evening, urging us on. "This time sing those words like you really believe them!" He waves his plumber's arms, inclines his head; his face glows. Hands are raised all over the room, hearts are focused on that inner reality—very inner. Yet we are together in our leaning—leaning into the holy, leaning into mystery. And, eyes closed, we sing the words as if we really mean them. . . . I am most interested in Buddy Ellison's unbounded theatrics by which he draws from his choir a true and holy song.[5]

Leonel L. Mitchell writes,

> Religious ritual is not always empty of meaning . . . and Christianity is not alone among world religions in seeing external actions as the necessary means of conveying and expressing interior realities. Love, whether of God or of the girl next door is all but impossible to express except through outward symbolic action, that is, through ritual acts. The same is true of friendship, respect, or, for that matter, hatred or contempt. We kiss, shake hands, shake our fist, turn our backs.[6]

Actions. Theatrics.

We might teach ourselves to use our facial expressions and our physical gestures by practicing them privately in front of a mirror so that, when we preach, they will come naturally and unconsciously.

Frown. Remain placid. Purse our lips. Raise an eyebrow. Arms held low. Arms in flight—always exhibiting the various moods of our stories. Incline our heads. Vary the tones of our voices. In his 1915 letter to Walter Prichard Eaton, Robert Frost says, "I have tried to see what I could do with boasting tones and quizzical tones and shrugging tones . . . and forty eleven other tones."[7] In the same way, there are "forty eleven" tones of voice by which we enhance the impact of our stories.

Preachers can switch from glee to solemnity. We can flash our eyes with excitement or else with a fatherly or motherly consolation during, say, a memorial service preached in front of those who are grieving for the beloved one whom they have lost.

Preachers are actors.

The preacher is not static.

—John Killinger, *Fundamentals of Preaching*

Ritual and worship.

The Native Americans' Sun Dance is a form of worship and a supreme example of the joining of motion with meaning. The dancers enter the Sun Dance circle precisely when the sun peeps over the eastern horizon and shoots its first fiery darts. They dance to the rhythmic sounds of their eagle-bone whistles—the start of their theatrics.

The ritual starts on Thursday and ends at noon on Sunday.

Early in the week, the leader selects the cottonwood tree that will be made sacred. On Wednesday, the tree is cut down and caught, as it must not touch the ground. Then it is carried from its place and into the sacred circle and planted upright in the center.

Those who have pledged to dance the next day tie the ends of long, colorful cords around the trunk of the cottonwood. Each dancer's cord ends in two loops.

Every action has its meaning.

To dance clockwise—"sunwise"—within the circle is to be encompassing the universe, and the tall cottonwood is the world's pole.

In the middle of Thursday morning, one of the dancers lays himself belly down on buffalo hide beside the tree. Two red circles have been painted on his chest. His plastic cord has been unraveled, its two loops also lying beside the tree.

Now the Sun Dance leader kneels down. He picks up two sharp skewers and pierces the flesh within the circles, then hooks the loops of this dancer's cord around the skewers.

The dancer stands. He is led four times quickly around the universal circle. After that, he starts to honor the sacred tree. He dances to it and puts his forehead against its trunk, and then he dances back to his place inside the arbor. He leans back until the skewers have pulled on his skin, looking like two cones. He does this three times.

At the fourth time, he turns and races away from the tree. Just as his cord has reached its limit, the dancer leaps. He whirls around and faces the tree, and the skewers snap free, and the cord zings back at the tree, and the dancer lands on his feet in a kind of ecstasy, and his wounds leak only a little blood.

Motion and meaning.

Black Elk says, "When we go to the center of the hoop, we all cry, for we should know that anything born into this world which you see about you must suffer and bear difficulties. We are now going to suffer at the center of the sacred hoop, and by doing this may we take upon ourselves much of the suffering of our people."[8]

18

Motion and Meaning II

Shakespeare's Hamlet explains how an actor ought, and ought not, to perform. Having just listened to an actor's bombastic declamation, Hamlet criticizes that actor's shameful, "dull and muddy-mettled" bluster:

> *But in a fiction, in a dream of passion,*
> *Could force his soul so to his own conceit*
> *That from his working all his visage wann'd,*
> *Tears in his eyes, distraction in 's aspect,*
> *A broken voice, and his whole function suiting*
> *With forms to his conceit? and all for nothing!*
> *For Hecuba!* (Hamlet, act two, scene two)

In act three, scene two, however, Hamlet offers the right way to act:

> Speak the speech, I pray you, as I pronounced it to you, trippingly on the tongue: but if you mouth it, as many of your players do, I had as lief the town-crier spoke my lines. Nor do not saw the air too much with your hand thus, but use all gently; for in the very torrent, tempest, and, as I may say, the whirlwind of your passion, you must acquire and beget temperance that may give it smoothness. O, it offends me to the soul to hear a robustious periwig-pated fellow tear a passion to tatters, to very rags, to split the ears of the groundlings.

Even our smallest gesture, our smallest twitch when we're telling a story, can have a considerable effect on our congregations. Eric Bentley examines the movement of an actor's eyes:

> Acting . . . has come to concentrate itself in the eyes. . . . A look is more dynamic as it is beginning to happen than when it actually happens. . . . As between persons [that is, between the preacher and the congregation], a look has its consummation when it is returned. The meeting of eyes constitutes a kind of center of human communication. The contact is more personal than a touch.[1]

With regard to how the playwright Eugene O'Neill's actors are to act, and how to turn their motions into meaning, he writes long, detailed, and specific stage directions. This brief piece is from his *Mourning Becomes Electra*. What's written in the parentheses is his own:

> Lavinia: (*with a stifled cry*) Orin! (*There is no answer but the sound of the study door being shut. She starts to run after him, stops herself, then throws herself into Peter's arms, as if for protection against herself and begins to talk volubly to drown out thought.*) Hold me close, Peter! Nothing matters but love, does it? That must come first! No price is too great, is it? Or for peace! One must have peace—one is too weak to forget—no one has the right to keep anyone from peace! (*She makes a motion to cover her ears with her hands.*)[2]

O'Neil's stage directions are too highly detailed for our sermons. But we can imitate them, turning them into shortish generalities of our own. And note the em dashes in his dialogue.

They indicate how actors ought to speak their lines, pausing for effect—to meditate or to signal a shift in the actors' attitudes.

The eminent critic Harold Bloom writes in a foreword to O'Neill's *A Long Day's Journey into Night* that O'Neill's dialogue ("Tyrone's petulant outbursts") is "considerably less eloquent than the stage directions."[3]

The importance of well-placed movement in preaching should not be underestimated. To move *is* to speak, sometimes more eloquently than with words. The script is important, but how we present the script may communicate meaning beyond the words.

19

The Entrance

Rev. David Wacker stood 6'4" tall. His arms were muscular and rangy. He could have played halfback on the seminary's football team, but he chose basketball. In the middle of a jump below the basket, Wacker could extend his right arm behind himself, catch one-handed and in midleap a high pass, then windmill his arm up and over, stuffing the ball—and all this in a single motion.

Wacker was my senior pastor at Redeemer Lutheran Church in Evansville, Indiana. He had a loud voice and a horsey laugh. When he entered the pulpit, he would lick his thumbs and yank up his cincture. The effect of these actions caused his congregation to see him as an athlete about to throw himself into a game.

Likewise, the manners and the motions by which we preachers enter our platforms or our chancel stage sets can communicate a great deal about the attitudes we will assume while preaching.

A quick step up the church's aisle, greeting our members and smiling as we come, may indicate a free and cheerful generosity.

Or a slow, portentous step, heads bowed, piety held between the flats of our ecclesiastical and possibly praying hands, can indicate a solemn (or posed?) attitude.

Certain high-liturgical churches initiate their worship services with a processional entrance behind a cross held high, betokening a formal ceremony.

Are the expressions on our faces benevolent? Or craggy? Perhaps we ought to consider the atmosphere our preaching will breathe into the sanctuary.

The role and the theatrical characters who we prepare to enact on a Sunday morning might be like one of the characters in an Uncle Remus story, genial and folksy, humorous and down-to-earth. Or we may choose to tell our stories in the character of Moses, who came down the mountain carrying the twin tablets of the law. When he saw the people running riot and worshipping a golden calf, he smashed the tablets and raised a voice of accusation: "You have sinned a great sin!" (Exod 32:30).

Be careful not to become legalistic. We may, of course, have to call a member (even the whole congregation?) to account for a transgression. But not in the manner of Moses—rather, in the manner of Jesus when he said, "Go and sin no more" (John 8:11 NKJV).

Or what if we choose to be Hermit the Frog? "It's not easy being a preacher."

Or, better yet, the character named Christian in John Bunyan's *The Pilgrim's Progress*.

Or Francis of Assisi, who saw a person with leprosy beside the road, a man whose face was one disgusting sore. He dismounted, and went to the leper, and kissed his hideous cheek.

These are only a few examples of the personhoods that we plan to take on when we enter the pulpit. They will define the purposes of our sermons, the who *we* are and the needs (the blessings or the judgments) of our congregations.

Recalling Eric Bentley's advice, I suggest that our eyes can establish a relationship with our people. After they have read and interpreted the cast of our eyes and our expressions, they will know right from the beginning what joy, what goodwill, what caution, what calling to account this relationship is to be.

John Killinger again:

> Watch the congregation. See and feel their reactions. Preach to those reactions. Lighten your tone when they find the going too heavy. Deepen it when they are smiling and in a good mood. Play to their needs and feelings as if you were a skilled actor or musician, sensitive to the invisible strands joining you to them in a great communal enterprise.[1]

20

Preacher as Actor, Sermon as Play Script

Just as preachers need to be aware of their physical presence in the worship setting and how their body language works in concert with their words, here we pull back the curtain on the preacher as actor and envision how the sermon can function as a play script. Jana Childers asks,

> What is it that makes a sermon work, fly, come to life, have zing, take wing, tear the place up? What gets a sermon up off the page, across the tops of the pews, and down into people's insides? What gives preaching transconscious appeal—the kind of impact that affects not just cerebrum but cerebellum too? What is the difference between that kind of sermon and the one that seems to dribble down the front of the pulpit and out into the aisles?[1]

The Voice

Jana Childers again: "Not only is the voice the preacher's most powerful tool, it is his or her most personal."[2]

My baritone voice is mine. The perfectly modulated voice of my pastor, Erica Gibson-Even, is hers. The telling of our tales, therefore, strikes different tones and different responses in our listeners' insides.

More generally, we pastors ought to know the effects of the sounds of our vowels. Their tones make a difference: a high happiness or a low melancholy.

The tongue is a muscle. The mouth is like the bell of a trumpet, projecting various sounds, and the lips shape the music of those sounds.

The following are two examples:

The following "ah" sounds—two syllables, stressed and unstressed—bespeak a child's exaggerated humor:

I'd clobber those robbers
Until they slobbered
And all their teeth decayed.
    W. M. W.

Or the spoken "O" (lips rounded, mouth hollow, the tongue bunched in the back of the mouth) can communicate sorrow:

"O my son Absalom, my son, my son Absalom" (2 Sam 18:33 KJV).

Read out loud Robert Frost's poem "Bereft." Listen to his "O" sounds and feel the effect of their repetition:

Where had I heard this wind before
Change like this to a deeper roar?
What would it take my standing there for,
Holding open a restive door,
Summer was past and day was past.
Somber clouds in the west were massed.
Out in the porch's sagging floor. . . .
Something sinister in the tone
Told me my secret must be known:
Word that I was in the house alone
Somehow must have gotten abroad,

Word I was in my life alone,
Word that I had no one left but God.[3]

The "O" sounds befit the sorrow of a man lonely and isolated.

Jerome Rockwood writes, "The actor's voice and body are his instrument, a sensitive instrument which must respond to the most subtle nuances of thought and feeling."[4]

When a portion of our stories rams forward (excited, at a quick speed, or at a conflict between characters), actors will—and pastors can—shorten their sentences and speak with quick punches:

Nasur, nassur,
Hump.
Eoho, eoho, roll away!
We aint agwine t' wait until the Judgment day!

God's body's got a soul,
Bodies like to roll the soul,
Can't blame God if we don't roll,
Come on, brother, roll, roll![5]

On the other hand, when the story is as peaceful as a morning mist floating over a still and windless lake, our voice tones can embrace our congregations with a music as gentle as a lullaby. But we shouldn't speak in flat and lifeless tones.

Rather, listen to a poem in which Emily Dickinson affirms the life of a poetic line:

A word is dead
When it is said,
Some say.

I say it just
Begins to live
That day.[6]

Frederick Buechner writes, "Words not only convey something, but *are* something. . . . [They] have color, depth, texture of their own, and the power to evoke vastly more than they mean."[7]

Action

I've spoken about this before, but it bears repeating. Various gestures will abet a story, making it visible, as it were, and causing a congregation to see and to experience it. Raising our arms can communicate joy, or something like triumph, or else a reaching up to heaven, where Jesus sits at the right hand of God.

To open our hands with our palms turned down and our arms both lifted and extended bestows a blessing on our people. Or as Jesus might have done at the beginning of his teaching ("Blessed are the poor in spirit . . ."), so we can do, inviting our congregations to enter into a personal community with us.

If we practice these gestures and many others in private, we'll be able to feel their differing effects within ourselves and thereby to know how our people will feel them when they are listening to our preaching.

Lay a finger to our lips? "Hush. Pay attention. I'm going to tell you something important."

Put that finger to the sides of our noses: "Let me think a while."

Pace. Stop. Turn to the congregation. The gesture might indicate a new paragraph, or a new topic, or the next chapter in our story.

We could walk across our stages like a patriarch, like a matriarch, and without words but by that walk alone gently ask for obedience.

I wonder if any of us has some bodily characteristic that cannot help but be noticed? My chin is like a clipper ship cutting through the waters. My jaw is wide and as strong as the jawbone of an ass with which Samson killed a thousand. I'm exaggerating, of course. Nevertheless, these characteristics could use a comment or two. And they are not unlike Cyrano de Bergerac's own exaggerations:

> Possibly you find [my nose] just a trifle large. . . .
>
> > Know that I glory in this nose of mine,
> > For a great nose indicates a great man. . . .
> > 'Tis a rock—a crag—a cape—
> > A cape? Say rather, a peninsula!⁸

Once more, I suggest that we ask a member of our congregation to videotape us while we're preaching on any given Sunday morning and then watch that video in private. Watch it over and over again. Speed it up to see how silly we seem to be.

Watching is seeing. Seeing is knowing. And knowing is the beginning of change.

When Barack Obama began to campaign for the presidency, his wife joined the campaign by speaking on the stump. But Michelle's gestures were ineffective. The people liked her well enough, but she wasn't moving them to *act*.

David Axelrod saw the fault. He videotaped her and told her to watch the tape with the sound turned down. Thus was she was able to recognize the fault of her gestures. So Michelle spent a period of time—sometimes in front of a mirror—practicing to make her gestures more effective, more personable, more persuasive. She became a friend of the assembled people, speaking with a conviction that convinced them to put their trust in, to campaign for, and to vote for Barack.

The Walk

Whether we preachers stand in our pulpits to tell our stories or whether we walk across our stages, our motions should conform to the moods and the rhythms, the passions and the progressions, of the story. Both are one. They are one and the *same* action.

Walking at a slow pace while looking at our congregations can bespeak a parental affection. A slack and lingering step with, perhaps, our lips rounded to a small hole as if we were blowing a silent whistle can prepare the people to experience an intimacy between ourselves and them.

A faster pace, matching a faster and more exciting action passage in a tale, can cause the hearts of the members of our congregations to beat at a ticktock speed: "What's coming? What is he, she, about to say?"

And what does it mean when we set our feet foursquare on the stage? Or fold our arms across our chests? Or plant a fist on our hips, just as a mother might when cooking at her stove?

Place a chair on the stage. Sit in it. Lean forward. Speak as to children.

Preachers Reading Aloud

These suggestions are my own. Take them or leave them as you wish.

When I'm reading the Gospel lesson aloud, I keep my eyes always down on the passage before me. I do this because at this point in the worship service, my relationship is not with the congregation. It is with God.

Neither do I interrupt my reading by looking up and down, up and down, up to the congregation and down to the Scripture. It breaks the rightful and faithful God-me relationship by trying to establish a me-people relationship. Moreover, this flicking of my eyes might fail because it's often too brief and too vacant to communicate anything at all.

Jana Childers alerts us to another futile gesture: "One of the most common complaints of listeners is that the speaker trails off at the ends of sentences."[9]

There are some preachers who, when reading aloud the manuscripts of their sermons, glance down in order to remind themselves of their next paragraph and at the same time lower their voices so softly that the congregation can scarcely hear and understand what they're saying.

And if they read their entire sermon, the relationship is not at all with their people. Instead, it is something like a relationship between their present selves and their past selves who had written their sermon during the week before.

Yet we have several ways to bring our sermons and our stories to life.

John Killinger writes that he "jotted down a quick list of key moves or ideas in the sermon, printing in heavy letters the things that had given me most trouble in mastering the sermon. I rarely consult my notes when preaching. Most people think I have none."[10]

Another way is much more difficult. This is to preach without notes and without a manuscript at all.

Some of us might memorize our sermons word for word. But that makes for a rigid performance and an inability to read our people's emotions. Nor can we vary our word-for-word stories.

Rather than memorizing the words, I suggest another way to set ourselves free is to shift *our* performances according to our people's moods and emotions: joy for joy, unhappiness for unhappiness, yearning for yearning, unspoken questions for spoken answers, holidays for holidays. This is an altogether different kind of memorization. It is to memorize, as it were, chunk by chunk.

Let's say that my sermon consists of three parts. I associate each part with three rooms in my house. None of us has trouble remembering the rooms in our houses. They are so familiar that we needn't give them a second thought.

Part one: I'm in my living room sitting comfortably in front of a fire in my fireplace. Framed pictures of my family hang on the walls. A bookcase. A piano. My wife's green and growing plants in the bay window.

It's easy to associate the pictures with descriptions of my story's characters and the living room with the setting of my story. And the theme of the first part of my sermon is the genial atmosphere in my living room. Right now, I don't have to think about the next room in which my next chunk waits for me. It will be there even while I'm busy talking about that first chunk.

Part two: next, I'm in the kitchen with new associations.

Part three: and finally, I'm in my bedroom. Jerome Rockwood writes,

> We remember things through our five senses. After you have *seen* everything in that dingy room, try to recall what things *felt* like—the worn, rough fabric on the sofa, the cheap stuffing sticking through, the uneven wooden floor underfoot. What did you *hear?* Was there a radio blaring next door? A dripping water tap? And what about *smells?* Was there any cooking going on? Was there a musty odor from lack of ventilation?[11]

Costumes

Gary Sloan writes, "So consider what kind of clothes your character might be wearing."[12]

A preacher's costume might be a tailored suit and a tie and hair well groomed: "Trust me. Trust my preaching as you would trust a trustworthy banker. I won't lead you wrong."

A turtleneck and slacks? "I'm your friend. I am your companion."

A flowing black robe with three hash marks around its loose sleeves—a pastor looking for all the world like an academician.

Liturgical garments—a clerical collar signifies the authority that was granted us by our ordination.

The colors of our stoles indicate the times, the seasons of the church year: blue for Advent, white for the days of Christmas, green for the Sundays in Epiphany, purple for Lent, white or gold for the day of the resurrection, red for Pentecost. And green for the ordinary Sundays, those that follow Pentecost. And every color matches the meanings of the seasons.

Costumes reveal by sight what doesn't have to be spoken.

Music

Music accompanies movies and television shows. Staged musicals, likewise, change with their narratives.

Our music accompanies the various (changing) parts of the worship services.

Luther D. Reed writes, "New forces which [Luther] released enriched the services of the church with hymns, chorales, and choir music of high devotional and artistic importance."[13]

When we sing hymns, we and the members of our congregations turn our voices into musical instruments. Our harmonies make us a single, faithful community. We are the music of the spheres. We sing praises to our God: "Crown him with many crowns, the Lamb upon his throne."

Our songs enact our trust:

Blessed assurance, Jesus is mine!
Oh, what a foretaste of glory divine.

They define our pilgrimage journeys:

Just a closer walk with thee,
Grant it, Jesus is my plea. . . .
I am weak, but thou art strong.

We sing hymns for the resurrection:

My Lord, what a morning;
My Lord, what a morning;
Oh, my Lord, what a morning
When the stars begin to fall.

And we sing hymns of lament:

In deepest night, in darkest days,
When harps hung, so songs we raise.

Such congregational music can express the feelings of a worshipping congregation.

The music of deep-throated organ pipes can lay down a foundation for preludes and hymns and psalm tones. The high, tweedling pipes can ascend from that foundation to soar with a heavenly birdsong. Pianos laugh and cause our hearts to dance or carry us along on the current of the Negro National Anthem: "Lift every voice and sing till earth and heaven ring . . ."

Guitars pluck and strum: "Shine, Jesus, shine, fill this land with the Father's glory!" Or "Jesu, Jesu, fill us with your love . . ." Or "Our God is an awesome God . . ."

Choirs clap and sway: "We've come this far by faith, leaning on the Lord . . ."

Quakers worship without music, and yet their thoughts and their silent meditations can be the unheard music of their prayers of patience and expectation.

Architecture

The sanctuaries of liturgical churches, or the churches with high platforms and vast assembly halls, or small churches with microphones and loudspeakers, or churches that worship behind storefronts on an inner-city street—each of these is the theater wherein we tell and enact our stories.

It is well for us to know how to use these interior spaces, the furniture, the windows and ceilings, the long cloth and colorful banners hanging on their walls, the weather outside and the weather inside the church. Hot? Humid? A scarcely moving air? Women fanning their faces? Or else on the winter days when our feet grow cold?

Does a morning sunshine flood our churches, casting a bright light on the faces of the people sitting in their pews? Then let us raise our voices in a sunlit glory.

Once, when I was preaching a Good Friday sermon in the vast and clear-windowed Chapel of the Resurrection in Valparaiso University, the outside clouds turned black. I don't remember what I'd been saying when a sudden flash of lightning struck down, lightning flashes that stuttered the earth, followed by a thunderclap. But because I'd memorized my sermon chunk by chunk, I was able to react to the weather's performance. I *had* to do so because all the people in the sanctuary forgot my preaching and could think of nothing else.

Boom! I made that storm a part of my sermon, thereby giving it meaning by referring to the heavy darkness and the earthquake that attended Christ's Good Friday death.

All of us can do the same when some small thing interrupts the smooth flow of our preaching. A baby's insistent crying? An organist's bumping of an accidental note in the middle of the service?

Look out through a church's clear windows and imagine not only that our churches are set in the natural world but also that our people are worshipping within the limitless universe.

Once, long ago, Judean priests taught that Jerusalem was in the center of the earth, and that the temple was in the center of the earth's circle, and that the ark of the covenant was itself the central point of all creation.

When telling a biblical tale in a church with stained glass windows, we might give place and personhood to one of its characters: Elijah ascending in a fiery chariot, Saint Peter with the keys of the kingdom, the Holy Spirit descending in the form of a dove, the Virgin Mary.

Gordon W. Lathrop in his *Holy Ground: A Liturgical Cosmology* writes, "Let the connections to the earth and the sky be an important consideration—demonstrated by honesty in the use of local materials, by the utilization of arts that recall the lines of connection that run out from this assembly, perhaps by *clear windows* that allow the earth-location of the assembly to be seen from within the building."[14]

We can put to use the architecture of our sanctuaries. The interiors of our churches are our theaters. Let preachers adjust their voices to the breadth and the depth of the theater's space. They stand under the theater's lights. They can refer to beams in the ceilings, or to the banners that hang on the walls like victorious flags, or to the chancel's steps as though they were Jacob's ladder.

A minister might start his or her sermon at the back of the sanctuary, then walk up the aisle to the swelling sound of the organ, thereby increasing the tension or else the wonder of what is about to begin.

What person could *not* feel in his or her bones the power of the tale to come?

My final thought regarding the church's architecture comes from Robert W. Jenson's *Essays in Theology of Culture*. He takes a completely different view of the space, the theater in which a play is enacted. His is a spiritual space:

> Space is precisely the present [itself] as against the past and the future. . . . Catholics have built holy theaters for viewing the sacred act, with the stage up front as the location for the Presence and an auditorium for the worshipers; Protestants have built holy lecture halls for hearing the sacred discourse, with the lecture desk as the holy place up there and with sound rather than sight as the bridge between the two locations; and Lutherans and some others have made a clumsy combination of the two. . . . The present reality of this God, his being now for us, is therefore not a quasi-spatial nearness but rather the *event* of this word that opens the future being spoken. . . . The space provided for the worship of this God, for his presence, must be a space for this action, for the telling and acting out of the gospel. It must, that is, be wholly a stage.[15]

We have walked a long road together, you and I, but it isn't finished until the story is told. Our relationship has been you and I. Hereafter, it will be with those who hear us. Go with God.

—Walt

Notes

Prologue

1 Jana Childers, *Performing the Word: Preaching as Theater* (Abingdon, 1998), 57.
2 Robert G. Hughes and Robert Kysar, *Preaching Doctrine for the Twenty-First Century* (Augsburg Fortress, 1997), 12.
3 Bruno Forte, *The Portal of Beauty: Towards a Theology of Aesthetics*, trans. David Glenday and Paul McPartlan (Wm. B. Eerdmans, 2008), 105.
4 Brenda Miller and Suzanne Paola, *Tell It Slant* (McGraw-Hill, 2005), 4.

Chapter 1

1 Vladimir Nabokov, *Lectures on Literature*, ed. Fredson Bowers (Harvest/HBJ, 1990), 4.
2 T. S. Eliot, "A Dialogue on Dramatic Poetry," in *Selected Essays* (Harcourt, Brace & World, 1960), 36.
3 Bruno Bettelheim, *The Uses of Enchantment* (Vintage Books, 1976), 24.

Chapter 2

1 Bettelheim, *Uses of Enchantment*, 53–54.
2 Jean Piaget, *The Child's Conception of the World*, trans. Joan and Andrew Tomlinson (Littlefield, Adams, 1963), 173.
3 Piaget, 223.
4 Piaget, 223 (italics mine).
5 Coleman Barks, trans., *The Soul of Rumi: A Collection of Ecstatic Poems* (HarperSanFrancisco, 2001), 16.

Chapter 3

1. Albert Ernest Fleming, trans., *Rainer Maria Rilke: Selected Poems* (Methuen, 1985), 209. Reprinted by permission.
2. Martin Buber, *I and Thou*, trans. Walter Kaufman (Charles Scribner's Sons, 1970), 53–54.

Chapter 4

1. Bettelheim, *Uses of Enchantment*, 118.
2. Selma G. Lanes, *Down the Rabbit Hole* (Atheneum, 1971), 71.
3. Matt 21:33–44; Mark 12:1–11; Luke 20:9–19.

Chapter 5

1. See Gen 32.
2. Quoted in *The Week*, December 11, 2020.

Chapter 6

1. Louis Dupré, *Symbols of the Sacred* (Wm. B. Eerdmans, 2000), 43.
2. Robert Frost, *The Complete Poems of Robert Frost* (Holt, Rinehart & Winston, 1964), vi.
3. William Stafford, *Writing the Australian Crawl* (University of Michigan Press, 1978), 24–25.
4. Stafford, 25.
5. Louis Ginzberg, *The Legends of the Jews*, trans. Henrietta Szold (Jewish Publication Society of America, 1909), vii.

Chapter 7

1. Hans Christian Andersen, *The Complete Fairy Tales and Stories*, trans. Erik Christian Haugaard (Doubleday, 1974), 306.
2. James Weldon Johnson, *God's Trombones: Seven Negro Sermons in Verse* (Viking, 1927), 17.
3. Herbert Anderson and Edward Foley, *Mighty Stories, Dangerous Rituals* (Jossey-Bass, 1998), 3.
4. Eugene L. Lowry, *The Sermon* (Abingdon, 1997), 60.

5　T. S. Eliot, *Selected Essays* (Harcourt, Brace & World, 1932), 353.
6　T. S. Eliot, "Religion and Literature," in Eliot, *Selected Essays*, 350.

Chapter 8
1　Bettelheim, *Uses of Enchantment*, 46.
2　As quoted in John Killinger, *Fundamentals of Preaching*, 2nd ed. (Fortress Press, 1996), 132–33.
3　Emmanuel Kant, *Observations on the Feeling of the Beautiful and Sublime*, trans. J. T. Goldtwait (University of California Press, 1960), 52.
4　Julian of Norwich, *Revelations of Divine Love*, quoted in Kant, *Observations*, 52.
5　Johnson, *God's Trombones*, 6.

Chapter 9
1　St. Ambrose of Milan, *The Confessions of St. Augustine*, trans. John K. Ryan (Doubleday, 1960), 43.
2　Text from *Lutheran Service Book: Pastoral Care Companion* (Concordia, 2007), xviii.
3　Carmen Bernos De Gasztold, "The Parrot," in *The Creatures' Choir*, trans. Rumer Godden (Penguin, 1970), 102.

Chapter 11
1　From Karen Saupe, ed., *Middle English Marian Lyrics* (Western Michigan University, 1998), 124.

Chapter 12
1　From William Griffin, trans., *Sermons to the People* (Image Books, 2002), 131.
2　Thomas W. Talley, *Negro Folk Rhymes: Wise and Otherwise* (Macmillan, 1922; Project Gutenberg, 2008), 109, https://www.gutenberg.org/files/27195/27195-h/27195-h.htm#Page_14.
3　Selma G. Lanes, *The Art of Maurice Sendak* (Harry N. Abrams, 1980), 85.

4 Select verses of the poem from *A College Book of Modern Verse*, ed. James K. Robinson and Walter B. Rideout (Row, Peterson, 1958), 388.

Chapter 13
1 Herman G. Stuempfle Jr., "Bring Peace to Earth Again," in *Evangelical Lutheran Worship* (Augsburg Fortress, 2006).

Chapter 14
1 Ginzberg, *Legends of the Jews*, ix.
2 Frederick A. Niedner, "Rachel's Lament," *Word & World* 22, no. 4 (Fall 2002): 406-14.

Chapter 15
1 Killinger, *Fundamentals of Preaching*, 58.
2 Saupe, *Middle English Marian Lyrics*, 153.
3 William B. McClain, *Come Sunday: The Literature of Zion* (Abingdon, 1990), 68.

Chapter 16
1 Leonel L. Mitchell, *The Meaning of Ritual* (Morehouse-Barlow, 1997), 12-14.
2 James Burge, *Heloise and Abelard: A Twelfth-Century Love Story* (Profile Books, 2003), 36.
3 Helen Hosier, *Jonathan Edwards: The Great Awakener* (Barbour, 1999), 78, 82.

Chapter 17
1 Flannery O'Connor, *Mystery and Manners: Occasional Prose*, ed. Robert and Sally Fitzgerald (Farrar, Straus & Giroux, 1969), 31.
2 John Gardner, *The Art of Fiction* (Vintage Books, 1983), 46.
3 St. Augustine, quoted in Childers, *Performing the Word*, 28.
4 David H. C. Read, quoted in Killinger, *Fundamentals of Preaching*, 166.

5   Childers, *Performing the Word*, 143.
6   Mitchell, *Meaning of Ritual*, 13.
7   In Timothy Steele, "'Across the Spaces of the Footed Line': The Meter and Versification of Robert Frost," in *Cambridge Companion to Robert Frost* (Cambridge University Press, 2001; Cambridge Companions Online, 2006), 690–91, https://epdf.pub/the-cambridge-companion-to-robert-frost-cambridge-companions-to-literature.html.
8   Black Elk, *The Sacred Pipe*, recorded and edited by Joseph Epes Brown (University of Oklahoma Press, 1953), 85.

Chapter 18
1   Eric Bentley, *The Life of the Drama* (Atheneum, 1967), 167.
2   Eugene O'Neill, *Mourning Becomes Electra* (Liveright, 1931).
3   Harold Bloom, foreword to *A Long Day's Journey into Night*, by Eugene O'Neill (Yale University Press, 1987), x.

Chapter 19
1   Killinger, *Fundamentals of Preaching*, 173.

Chapter 20
1   Childers, *Performing the Word*, 19.
2   Childers, 58.
3   Frost, *Complete Poems*, 317.
4   Jerome Rockwood, *The Craftsmen of Dionysus: An Approach to Acting* (Applause Books, 1966), 14.
5   Jean Toomer, "Cotton Song," in *The Black Poets*, ed. Dudley Randell (Bantam Books, 1971), 69.
6   Originally published in *The Complete Poems of Emily Dickinson* (Little, Brown, 1924). Accessed online at Emily Dickinson, "A Word Is Dead," Monadnock Valley Press, accessed August 11, 2021, https://monadnock.net/dickinson/word.html.
7   Frederick Buechner, quoted in William J. Bausch, *Storytelling: Imagination and Faith*, 5th ed. (Twenty-Third, 1984), 14.

8. Edmond Rostand, *Cyrano de Bergerac: A New Version in English Verse by Brian Hooker* (Henry Holt, 1951), 21, 38.
9. Childers, *Performing the Word*, 73.
10. Killinger, *Fundamentals of Preaching*, 67.
11. Rockwood, *Craftsmen of Dionysus*, 37.
12. Gary Sloan, *In Rehearsal* (Routledge, 2012), 194.
13. Luther D. Reed, *The Lutheran Liturgy* (Fortress, 1947), 80.
14. Gordon W. Lathrop, *Holy Ground: A Liturgical Cosmology* (Fortress, 2009), 173 (italics mine).
15. Robert W. Jenson, *Essays in Theology of Culture* (Wm. B. Eerdmans, 1995), 10ff.